DINNER WITH
Tennessee Williams

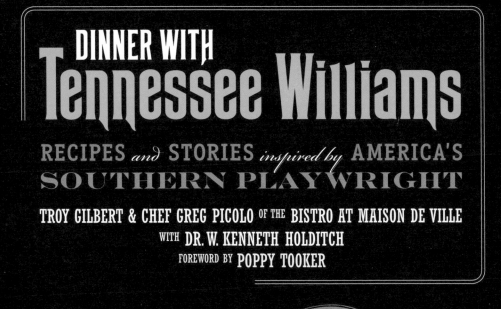

DINNER WITH
Tennessee Williams

RECIPES *and* STORIES *inspired by* AMERICA'S
SOUTHERN PLAYWRIGHT

TROY GILBERT & CHEF GREG PICOLO OF THE BISTRO AT MAISON DE VILLE

WITH DR. W. KENNETH HOLDITCH

FOREWORD BY POPPY TOOKER

GIBBS SMITH
TO ENRICH AND INSPIRE HUMANKIND

First Edition
15 14 13 12 11   5 4 3 2 1

Published by
Gibbs Smith
P.O. Box 667
Layton, Utah 84041

1.800.835.4993 orders
www.gibbs-smith.com

Designed by Debra McQuiston
Printed and bound in China
Gibbs Smith books are printed on either recycled, 100% post-consumer waste, FSC-certified
papers or on paper produced from sustainable PEFC-certified forest/controlled wood source.
Learn more at www.pefc.org.

Library of Congress Cataloging-in-Publication Data

Gilbert, Troy A.
  Dinner with Tennessee Williams : recipes and stories inspired by America's Southern
playwright / Troy Gilbert and Greg Picolo with W. Kenneth Holditch ; Foreword by Poppy
Tooker. — 1st ed.
    p. cm.
  ISBN 978-1-4236-2173-7
  1. Cooking, American—Southern style. 2. Cooking—Louisiana—New Orleans. 3. Williams,
Tennessee, 1911-1983. 4. Cookbooks. I. Picolo, Greg. II. Holditch, W. Kenneth. III. Title.
  TX715.2.S68G54 2011
  641.59763`35—dc22
                         2010048670

"Don't you just love those long rainy afternoons in New Orleans when an hour isn't just an hour—but a little piece of eternity dropped into your hands— and who knows what to do with it?"
— Tennessee Williams, *A Streetcar Named Desire*

CONTENTS

ACKNOWLEDGMENTS

At an early age, before I started working or showed any inclination, my grandfather, Julien Hardouin, an immigrant from Lyon, France, predicted that when I grew up I would become a chef. Although he did not live to see it, I am glad his insight came to fruition. I would also like to acknowledge the love of food and cooking that I have which was passed on to me by my mother, who was a great cook and the best improviser and utilization expert I ever knew.

I want to thank all the chefs who realized my potential and helped nurture my passion, above all Ciro Cuomo and Patty Queen. All of the cooks I have worked with over the years have guided me to achieve the high standards that have been the hallmark of my cooking at the Bistro, where I have had the pleasure of being executive chef for the past sixteen years.

Most importantly I need to thank Obie Chisholm, who has been my sous chef, best friend, and culinary confident for the past fourteen years. Thank you for every day and especially for all your assistance in the photo shoot of the dishes in this book.

I cannot thank Troy Gilbert enough for presenting me the opportunity to be a part of this project. He supported my ideas and gave me full creative license to reimagine the foods of Tennessee Williams. It has been a great experience working with him on this book.

A special thanks to Mike and Jaydine Maimone for when the restaurant was on the verge of shuttering after the storm; they stepped in and bought the Bistro and asked me to continue my role as executive chef.

Thanks to Dr. Kenneth Holditch for his insights, food references, and all the great stories about Tennessee Williams; it was most inspiring and invaluable.

Mostly I thank the great playwright Tennessee Williams for all of his amazing works and the abundance of food references that gave me so many ideas for the recipes. I can only hope that he would approve of my reimaginations.

—Greg Picolo

While my name may be on the credits for this book, absolutely none of it could have been accomplished if you subtract one name from the following contributors.

Paul Willis and Ellen Johnson with the New Orleans Tennessee Williams Literary Festival, both of whom immediately recognized the potential for this book and graciously accepted us into that special New Orleans world.

Obie Chisolm, Chef's hardworking and incredibly talented sous chef. I one day hope to become a regular at your own restaurant.

Jennifer Adams, our editor at Gibbs Smith Publishing, who did an amazing job while tackling this project under incredibly tight time constraints... one down, two more to go.

Gibbs Smith, our publisher who immediately understood and loved this project. His excitement for and knowledge of Tennessee Williams allowed us to move ahead rapidly through the process and have this book out in time for the centennial celebration of the playwright's birthday.

Alison Gootee whose artistic photography so perfectly brings to life the ideas we were conveying. Also, her patience in dealing with Greg and I during the long photo shoots in the late tropical New Orleans summer was astonishing.

Poppy Tooker is another one who immediately "got" this book. Her knowledge, enthusiasm and love for everything culinary in New Orleans is a great asset for the city and we are humbled by her agreeing to write the foreword for us.

Dr. Kenneth Holditch, the real scholarly force behind this project. Dr. Holditch's work not only added depth to this book, but it was fascinating to hear his stories and share in the breadth of his knowledge of the playwright.

Greg Picolo—what can I say but that Chef is the real genius behind this book. He understood exactly where I was going with the idea and his creations speak for themselves. Plus now I've got a ton of tasty food in my freezer.

Coincidences led us to the start of this project, hard work finished it and an amazing group of people who contributed came together and all share in the accomplishment of this book and a great chapter in our lives.

—Troy Gilbert

FOREWORD

I t's little wonder that Tennessee Williams loved New Orleans as he did. All of the elements that fueled his life and his art he found there in abundance. Fine food, intoxicating liquor, and the exoticism of the port city must have overwhelmed his senses at times; I know it still does mine.

On a walk though the Vieux Carre, past restaurants where Tennessee dined and drank, you feel as though he might still inhabit the streets of the French Quarter. New Orleanians love their ceremony and tradition almost as much as they love their food. That's why not much has changed at restaurants that now double as New Orleans's food museums, maintaining century-old menus and old-world service long abandoned in the rest of the world. The fountains still play in the Royal Street courtyard of Two Sisters; the remoulade at Arnaud's is the same spicy version Tennessee enjoyed, and, if you're lucky, Tennessee's favorite corner table—in the front window of Galatoire's Restaurant on Bourbon Street—is waiting for you. Order Tennessee's favorite trout meunière, and there's even a chance it will be served by an elderly waiter who once served the playwright.

Sadly, not everything of Tennessee's New Orleans remains.

The French Market is not the bustling real food market he so loved to frequent. Even more regrettable, his favorite market coffee stand, Morning Call, moved to the suburbs of Metairie years ago.

The glorious Royal Street food emporium Solari's is no more. Today, one of the Brennan's family bistros, Mr. B's, occupies the Solari's corner at Royal and Iberville. With a bit of imagination though, it's easy to envision Tennessee sipping a martini at the bar there.

But without a doubt, in today's New Orleans, Tennessee would most miss Marti's. Situated across the street from his last home on Dumaine Street, Marti's was so much more than a dining establishment to him.

Marti's Restaurant was the namesake of Marti Shambra, who opened his intimate bistro-style restaurant on the corner of Rampart and Dumaine in 1971. When asked if he had any previous restaurant experience Marti said, "None whatsoever. I was a lifeguard at the Fontainebleu, so I know how difficult it was to get a sandwich out of the kitchen." We can only imagine the friendship that developed between Tennessee and the young, handsome, ambitious Marti Shambra despite Tennessee's remark, "Poor man! He can hardly read!"

Marti's Restaurant operated as Tennessee's de facto home dining room. When he tired of the regular menu dishes the restaurant had became known for, like trout farci (a whole trout stuffed with a rich crabmeat dressing and finished with a brown butter meunière sauce), Marti himself would cook up the country-style mustard and turnip greens or the butter beans smothered with onions and bacon fat of Tennessee's Southern childhood table. Reportedly, Tennessee would drawl, "Pile some more of those turnip greens on the plate, please."

This book is certain evidence that Tennessee's muse is still at work in New Orleans. So many elements came together to make it happen that somehow, it seems the playwright had to have had a hand in its creation. The coincidences are just too numerous.

In 1938, Tennessee came to live in the New Orleans French Quarter for the first time. He settled into the third floor of a boarding house at 722 Toulouse Street, where his delicious explorations of the Crescent City began. Just across the street today, at 733 Toulouse, Chef Greg Picolo's Bistro at the Maison de Ville is where the magical convergence begins.

Greg Picolo and Tennessee Williams share many things, including a birthday, March 26th! In a New Orleans dialect that the playwright would love, Greg sometimes sounds as though he sprung from the pages of a Williams's play. I like to think of them together, sitting by the fountain's splashing waters in the Bistro's intimate courtyard. I know the two of them would have much to discuss.

Tennessee never dined at the Bistro at the Maison de Ville. The tiny jewel box of a restaurant opened in 1986, only three years after his death, but oh, how he would have loved it! Stepping in from the bustle of the street, the red leather banquettes and beveled glass mirrors reflect a Parisian air, but the food is decidedly the Louisiana Creole style he loved. Inspired by the bounty of the local land and water, Chef Greg delights in creating new dishes while honoring our classic culinary roots.

With a lifelong love of Tennessee's works, Greg was the perfect choice of chef to fancifully translate the beloved plays into artwork for the plate. Many wonderful experiences, both sweet and savory, await you between the pages of this book. All of your favorite characters and their favorite foods are here. Tuck into a bourbon-and-Coke-glazed double pork chop with Big Daddy. Share a little Southern Comfort with Blanche DuBois in the form of bread pudding. Chef Greg's recipes for Hoppin' John and Greens with Pickled Pork and Andouille Sausage are recreated exactly as Tennessee loved to eat them.

I hope this book inspires you to come to New Orleans in search of Tennessee. He's here waiting for you and I promise you the most delicious trip of your lifetime!

INTRODUCTION

I

n early 2006, I first sat down with Chef Greg Picolo over a glass of wine in the courtyard of his French Quarter restaurant to interview him regarding New Orleans's recent "troubles." He was one of the first chefs in a long list that I discussed the trials of restarting their restaurants while still vast swaths of the city lay in ruin and was devoid of nearly 80 percent of its citizenry.

What's amusing to me now with so much time having past is that no one ever truly understands the transformative process one might be going through, or for that matter an entire city or even something as simple as a recipe might go through, until you can stand there and finally see and taste where one now resides.

Nowhere in my mind on that quiet day in the courtyard surrounded by the Quarter was there even the remotest thought that Greg and I would be venturing together on a book project some four years later. Nor was I aware that Tennessee Williams had lived behind the doorway across the

courtyard that stared at us as we shared storm stories, peppered now and then with laughter.

In 2008, after turning in the manuscript for *New Orleans Kitchens* that I coauthored with Stacey Meyer, I sat down to a celebratory dinner with Gibbs Smith, our publisher, and I didn't blink when we were ushered to Tennessee Williams's table at Galatoire's.

Now with this manuscript completed, it doesn't surprise me in the least as I remember how Chef Greg was the first individual I thought of after I conceived of *Dinner with Tennessee Williams*. Greg's sense of humor, creativity, and New Orleans soul pointed him to me, and, lo and behold, he had a frequent patron of his restaurant who is a preeminent scholar of the playwright, Dr. Kenneth Holditch.

Coincidences led us to the start of this project, and what follows is a transformation of the food spiced throughout the work and life of Tennessee Williams—something which is so integral to his Southern upbringing and the city that he loved.

This book holds a reinvention of the old classics of New Orleans

restaurants as described in *Vieux Carre* and *A Streetcar Named Desire*; it's a riff off of the quintessential old Southern dishes of Big Daddy's birthday dinner in a *Cat on a Hot Tin Roof* and the dainty servings and glass of claret in *Summer and Smoke*. Chef Greg Picolo has immersed himself into the culinary dialect of Tennessee Williams and married these references or placed these flavors into new contexts while staying true to the ingredients and the plays.

It was an incredible journey to watch as Chef processed through the utilization of ingredients and spices that may or may not have been explicitly stated by the playwright to bang out massive tastes and subtle treatises of flavor that I have been able to easily reproduce in my home kitchen. This book is layered with discoveries of old recipes made new again.

Pairing these recipes with Dr. Holditch's detailed and nuanced writings on the culinary aspects of Tennessee Williams's writings and life, and we suddenly have a dream brought to life—one that I hope would, after reading, make the playwright walk out of the door and into the French Quarter to dine.

Left: *A Streetcar Named Desire* (1947–1949 Broadway) Play by Tennessee Williams Directed by Elia Kazan Shown: Playwright Tennessee Williams on the set of the original production at the Ethel Barrymore Theater

Right: *Camino Real* (1953 National Theatre, NY) Play by Tennessee Williams Directed by Elia Kazan Shown backstage, from left: Eli Wallach, Tennessee Williams, Elia Kazan

SOUTHERN COMFORT

Thomas Lanier Williams spent his early years in Mississippi, where he was born in Columbus on 26 March 1911. The next seven years, his extended family—his mother, Edwina Williams; Rose, his sister; and the Rev. and Mrs. Walter Dakins, his maternal grandparents—lived in Episcopal rectories in Columbus and Clarksdale, Mississippi, while his father, Cornelius Coffin Williams, traveled around the South selling Red Goose shoes. After Cornelius took a job in St. Louis and moved his family there, Tom occasionally returned to Clarksdale to stay with his grandparents in the Delta. Given the brevity of his time in Mississippi, it may seem surprising to what an extent the state marked him and his career, so much so that theatre critic John Quinn could write in 2005, "His gift was an ear for the poetic quality of the English language set to the lilt of the Delta dialect."

During the years of his Southern childhood, Tennessee Williams became accustomed to the traditional foods of the region. Whoever did the cooking for the Dakins and Williams household—it was most likely the grandmother or Ossie, who worked for several years for them—probably prepared meals in the traditional Southern mode. These would have included fresh garden vegetables in the spring, summer, and fall; canned in the winter. There would be the traditional Southern meat dishes—chicken and dumplings, fried chicken, fried or baked ham, pork chops, and roast beef. And of course, the obligatory desserts: pies, cakes, boiled custard, puddings, and cookies. All the above would have been washed down with sweetened iced tea, coffee, or milk. It must be noted, however, that Tennessee's grandparents, the Dakins, were from Ohio, and I do not presume to know what folks may eat there.

Because it was the custom in early decades of the twentieth century for parishioners to provide food for ministers and their families—even Episcopal rectors in the South were not well paid as some of Tennessee's letters to his grandfather attest—the Williams-Dakins household must have received, among their offerings, country hams, sausage, and fresh chickens, along with fresh produce and desserts, as a tribute from members of the parish. However, it is clear from those early letters that the Dakins raised their own chickens, at least in Clarksdale. Tommy Williams, in the Delta to stay with his grandparents in February 1920, wrote to his mother that Grand (as the children called their grandmother) had killed "fussy, the old Plymouth Rock" rooster to make "chicken salad and dumplings." Two weeks later, he wrote to his sister Rose that he "found fussys head in the back yard and gave it a nice burial," an appropriate action for the grandson of a rector.

IN *A STREETCAR NAMED DESIRE,* BLANCHE, LOOKING AROUND, FINDS A LIQUEUR:

"HERE'S SOMETHING. SOUTHERN COMFORT!

WHAT IS THAT I WONDER?... UMMM, IT'S SWEET, SO SWEET! IT'S TERRIBLY, TERRIBLY SWEET!"

TOWERS CORK & WOOD PENHOLDER PAT.

The Southern devotion to good food and, in some sectors, good drink, not surprisingly plays a major role in the plays of Williams, since he was one of the most Southern of authors. The dramatist's uncanny ability to seize a symbol in the most unlikely place is demonstrated in *A Streetcar Named Desire*, in the scene in which Blanche, looking around the Kowalski apartment for something she and Mitch can drink, finds a liqueur: "Here's something. Southern Comfort! What is that I wonder?. . . Ummm, it's sweet, so sweet! It's terribly, terribly sweet!" The words reflect ironically on the tragic events that soon will impact Blanche's fragile life. More often than not, his characters seem to experience Southern *dis*comfort, although they are always seeking a balm for their injured spirits. But for Tennessee, Southern comfort was a reality, particularly as exhibited in the character of his grandmother, whose visits from the Delta to St. Louis served as a balm for the exiled mother and children.

In one of his Delta plays, *Cat on a Hot Tin Roof*, Big Mama relies on an old Southern standard for judging good health:

Big Mama: Did you all notice the food [Big Daddy] ate at the table? Did you all notice the supper he put away? Why, he ate like a hawss! . . . Why, that man—ate a huge piece of cawn-bread with molasses on it! Helped himself twice to hoppin' john.

Margaret: Big Daddy loves hoppin' john.—We had a real country dinner.

Big Mama: Yair, he simply adores it! An' candied yams? That man put away enough food at that table to stuff a . . . field-hand!

Gooper: I hope he don't have to pay for it later on . . .

Big Mama: Why should Big Daddy suffer for satisfying a normal appetite?

"A real country dinner" is exactly what Tennessee himself liked, and in the 1970s, he frequented a restaurant in the French Quarter named Marti's where they would prepare for him mustard and turnip greens, peas and butter beans, seasoned with bacon fat. ("The Unsatisfactory Supper," a one-act play, contains a traditional Southern recipe for cooking greens: "A good mess of greens is a satisfactory meal if it's cooked with salt pork an' left on th' stove till it's tender, but thrown in a platter ha'f cooked an' unflavored, it ain't even fit for hog slops.")

In *Suddenly Last Summer*, George chastises his sister Catherine for her strange account of their cousin's death by altering an old, somewhat gross Southern adage: " . . . if you don't stop talking that crazy story, we won't have a pot to—cook greens in!" In yet another allusion to Southern fare in the same play, Catherine, confined to a mental institution, pleads with her mother to "give me written permission not to eat fried grits. I had yard privileges till I refused to eat fried grits."

I n Williams's plays, various characters express two diametrically opposing views of the relationship of the Southern woman and the kitchen. The notion that the place for her is in the kitchen functions in several plays, for example in *Summer and Smoke*, when Rev. Winemiller complains that Alma doesn't go out or do anything, she replies that she has "peeled the potatoes and shelled the peas and set the table for lunch," as if that is what the male of the family would expect from her. In "The Unsatisfactory Supper," Aunt Rose Comfort, a poor relation living with Archie Lee and Baby Doll, justifies her existence by doing the cooking. One night she forgets to light the stove to cook the greens, and when Archie Lee leaves his on the plate, she announces that she is going to cook "eggs Birmingham," but Archie, convinced that she is no longer useful as a cook, wants her removed to another relative's house. Amanda Wingfield in *The Glass Menagerie*, on the other hand, asserts that "I never could make a thing but angel food

Suddenly, Last Summer (1959) Directed by Joseph L. Mankiewicz Shown: French language poster

cake," a reflection of the image of her generation that Southern belles were intended to be ornamental, not practical.

On the other hand, determined to convince the Gentleman Caller that Laura is marriageable, Amanda insists that Laura has cooked the entire meal. One kitchen task Amanda, and other Southern ladies of various vintages in Tennessee's plays, can perform is to make lemonade. In "Twenty-Seven Wagons Full of Cotton," Flora makes Vicarro "a pitcher—of nice cold—lemonade!" to which she adds gin. In *The Glass Menagerie*, Amanda enters with a pitcher for her daughter and the Gentleman Caller, proclaiming the old doggerel:

Lemonade, lemonade
Made in the shade and stirred with a spade—
Good enough for any old maid!

And in *Summer and Smoke*, Alma Winemiller entertains her beau Roger Doremus with "a cut-glass pitcher of lemonade with cherries and orange slices in it, like a little aquarium of tropical fish."

Southern drinking customs receive considerable attention in the plays, as when Beulah remembers the "Dago's" wine garden, which was burned down when the owner sold liquor to blacks. Now the local purveyor of spirits in Two Rivers County is the bootlegger Ruby Lightfoot, and near the end of the play, Lady inquires if Ruby has delivered half pints for Seagrams for the opening of her new confectionery. "They all call for Seven-and-Sevens," she states, then asks her young clerk Val if he knows "how to sell bottle goods under the counter." Likewise, Chicken asks Myrtle, who has just married his half-brother Lot in *Kingdom of Earth* if she knows "the setup" and the naive Myrtle replies, "The only setup I know is in a dry state they'll serve you a setup for liquor but not the liquor," and Chicken, who is of mixed blood, says, "They don't sell me bottle liquor in this county but I can get it by the jug from a old colored man that brews a pretty good brew." Clearly Tennessee remembered hearing his elders talk about such things in his early years in Mississippi.

When they were living in Clarksdale in the second decade of the twentieth century, the Dakins, Edwina, and her two children would often take Sunday dinner at Moon Lake Casino in Dundee, operated at the time by a cousin of Rev. Dakins's, and liquor was certainly served there. At a lawn party in *Spring Storm* for the young socially prominent people of the town of Port Tyler (a thinly disguised Clarksdale), there is no liquor, but the elderly bartender has been instructed to hide a bottle and bring it out only to spike the drinks of the "older gentlemen."

In the little known *Kingdom of Earth*, Lot recalls of his mother that "Ev'ry afternoon about this time, Miss Lottie would take a glass of this Spanish sherry with a raw egg in it to keep her strength up. It would always revive her, even when she was down to eighty-two pounds . . . she called it her sherry flip. . . ." After Jane in *Vieux Carre* has her fashion drawings turned down, she says that "it left me too shattered to carry my portfolio home without a shot of Mataxas brandy at the Blue Lantern. . . ." After Alma has come to Dr. John Randolph's house in a panic in *Eccentricities of a Nightingale*, he gives her a drink and she "seizes the brandy glass," after which she proclaims that it "worked quickly. . . . I feel like a water-lily on a Chinese lagoon." And in *A Streetcar Named Desire*, Blanche asks Stella for a drink: "No Coke, honey, not with my nerves tonight! . . . Just water, baby, to chase it! You don't get worried, your sister hasn't turned into a drunkard. . . ." Similarly, Leona in *Small Craft Warning*, needs a restorative when she discovers that her lover is leaving, but the bartender has cut her off, so she asks Quentin to "order a double bourbon and pretend it's for you."

THE GLASS MENAGERIE

The "Eloquent" Oyster

"YOU'RE ELOQUENT AS AN OYSTER"

serves 6

6 medium-sized portobello
mushroom caps
1/2 cup extra virgin olive oil
Salt and pepper
2 cups chicken stock
4 tablespoons unsalted butter,
divided
1 small bulb fennel, diced
2 tablespoons Herbsaint
1 pound fresh spinach, cleaned
1 tablespoon + 2 teaspoons
minced garlic, divided
1/2 teaspoon nutmeg
1 can snails (approximately 30)
3 tablespoons chopped Italian
flat-leaf parsley
1/2 cup veal demi-glace*
24–36 raw Gulf oysters
6 thick slices Fontina cheese

This is available in specialty stores

Toss the mushroom caps with olive oil, salt, and pepper. On a hot grill, grill both sides of the caps until well marked. Place the caps on a sheet pan with high sides and cover with stock. Bake at 400 degrees F for 3–7 minutes or until tender; set aside.

Melt 3 tablespoons butter in a sauté pan and add fennel. Cook over low heat until tender, about 3–5 minutes. Add the Herbsaint and flame carefully. Add the spinach, 1 tablespoon garlic, nutmeg, and adjust seasoning with salt and pepper. Depending on how dry the spinach is, you may need to add a bit more stock. When the spinach is cooked, drain any excess liquid.

In a sauté pan, melt 1 tablespoon butter over medium heat. Add the snails, remaining garlic, parsley, demi-glace, and salt and pepper to taste. Heat the snails for 1–2 minutes only. Do not overcook.

Place the cooked mushroom caps bottom up in a 9 x 13-inch pan that has been coated with nonstick spray. Divide the oysters and snails evenly among the caps. Top with the spinach mixture. Bake for about 5–7 minutes at 450 degrees F in a preheated oven. Remove and place a slice of cheese on top of each stuffed cap and return to the oven. When the cheese has melted, after about 1 minute, remove mushroom caps from oven and serve.

Grilled Louisiana Shrimp and Coconut "Macaroons"

serves 6 to 8

SHRIMP AND COCONUT "MACAROONS"

2½ cups shredded unsweetened coconut
4 cups heavy cream
¼ teaspoon dark chili powder
⅛ teaspoon cayenne pepper
¼ teaspoon ground ginger
½ teaspoon garlic powder
1 teaspoon Chinese five-spice powder
1 teaspoon kosher salt
1 teaspoon fresh lime juice
1 egg, beaten
2 egg yolks, beaten
5 sheets packaged phyllo
8 tablespoons butter, melted
18 fresh jumbo Gulf shrimp
Salt and pepper
2 tablespoons extra virgin olive oil

VINAIGRETTE

Zest of 1 lime
Zest of 1 lemon
3 limes, juiced
1 teaspoon curry powder
1 teaspoon Sriracha or Tabasco
2 cloves garlic, minced
6 leaves fresh basil, chiffonade
1 tablespoon grainy Creole mustard
½ cup olive oil

Shrimp and Coconut "Macaroons" Combine the coconut, cream, spices, salt, and lime juice in a heavy-bottomed saucepan. Cook for 7–10 minutes or until the coconut is tender. Remove from heat and cool to room temperature.

Beat egg with the egg yolks and then add to the coconut mixture; let rest.

Brush the phyllo sheets generously with melted butter and shape sheets into cups. (The butter acts as a glue and will soften the phyllo so that it can be easily formed.) Place the cups on a sheet pan that has been sprayed with nonstick spray and bake at 450 degrees F for 4 minutes or until lightly browned. Remove cups from oven.

Spoon the coconut and egg mixture into the cups. Return sheet pan to the oven and bake an additional 5 minutes or until the mixture is firm.

Peel and devein the shrimp and season with salt and pepper. Toss with the olive oil and grill on a hot grill until pink, about 2–3 minutes per side. Do not overcook.

Vinaigrette To make the vinaigrette, combine all of the ingredients except the mustard and oil. Add the mustard and then drizzle in the oil; whip to make an emulsion.

To Serve Toss the grilled shrimp in the vinaigrette and place on top of the "macaroons." Serve.

Amanda's Smoked Salmon Loaf with Poached Eggs, Frisée, and Remoulade Blanc Topped with Toffika Caviar

serves 6

SMOKED SALMON LOAF
3 pounds raw fresh salmon
4 egg whites
1/4 teaspoon ground ginger
1 tablespoon lite soy sauce
1 teaspoon fresh lemon juice
Salt and pepper
1/4–1/2 teaspoon black smoked sea salt*
Remoulade Blanc (see below)
6 poached eggs
6 ounces Wasabi Toffika Caviar per serving*
Frisée for garnish

REMOULADE BLANC
1 1/2 cups good-quality mayonnaise
1 cup prepared horseradish
2 tablespoons Creole mustard
2 tablespoons fresh lemon juice
1 tablespoon Worcestershire
2 tablespoons chopped parsley
1 tablespoon capers (optional, but recommended)
Salt and pepper

POACHED EGGS
6 eggs
2 cups seasoned rice wine vinegar
Water

* This is available in specialty stores

Smoked Salmon Loaf In a food processor, blend the raw salmon until smooth, about 1 minute on high speed. Add the egg whites and pulse until incorporated. Add the ginger, soy sauce, and lemon juice. Add the salt and pepper to taste.

Remove the salmon mixture from the food processor and place in a terrine. Sprinkle the top with smoked sea salt. (Be careful not to add too much as this salt can be very strong and only gets stronger with cooking.) Cover terrine and place in a bain-marie or water bath. Bake in the oven for 7–12 minutes at 425 degrees F or until firm but still springy to the touch. Remove the lid and allow to cool.

Remoulade Blanc In a medium-sized bowl, combine all of the ingredients. Season with salt and pepper to taste; chill until ready to use.

Poached Eggs Fill a large saucepan with salted water and heat to a simmer. Add vinegar; this helps firm the whites and does not have an overpowering taste. Drop in each egg and allow to simmer for 13 minutes or until preferred doneness.

To Serve Arrange frisée on plates and top with generous slices of the salmon loaf. Place a poached egg on top of each plate and drizzle with the remoulade. Top with 1 ounce of caviar per dish and serve. (The caviar is optional, but highly recommended.)

Baton Aubergines

serves 6 to 8

1 loaf French bread, 2–3 days old
Peanut oil for frying
3 eggs, beaten
4 cups milk
2 large eggplants
Salt and pepper
6 cups all-purpose flour, seasoned
1 cup confectioners' sugar
1 cup grated Parmesan

Break French bread into medium-sized pieces. Preheat oven to 400 degrees F. When it reaches 400 degrees F, turn it off. Place bread pieces on a sheet pan and put in the oven. Allow bread to stay in the warm oven overnight. The next day, use a grater to grind toasted bread into very small crumbs.

In a fryer, the larger the better, heat the peanut oil to 375 degrees F. Make an egg wash by combining eggs and milk.

Peel the eggplants and slice into batons about $\frac{1}{2}$-inch square. Season with salt and pepper, and then dredge in the seasoned flour. Shake off excess flour and then dredge into the egg wash. Immediately toss in the breadcrumbs, covering completely. Prepare the breaded eggplant sticks only minutes before frying. Carefully place into the fryer. (If using a small fryer, do this in small batches.) Remove batons when golden brown. Drain on paper towels. Serve sprinkled with confectioners' sugar and grated Parmesan. Serve immediately.

CHEF to cook

The mistake that's often made with this dish is that the eggplant is sliced too long before it is fried. Slice just before breading and frying. This is a traditional Galatoire's dish, re-invented.

Angel Food Cake Pain Perdu with Hart Crane's Peppermint Sauce

serves 6 to 10

PAIN PERDU
2-inch-thick slices angel food cake
(purchased or your favorite recipe)
6 tablespoons butter
4 cups half-and-half
1½ cups sugar
3 eggs
1 tablespoon pure vanilla extract
1 teaspoon ground cinnamon
Hart Crane's Peppermint Sauce
(see below)

HART CRANE'S PEPPERMINT SAUCE
3 tablespoons unsalted butter
1 cup sugar
3 cups heavy cream
6 (regular-size) pulverized
peppermint Lifesavers
1 teaspoon pure vanilla extract
½ pound high-quality bittersweet
chocolate, finely chopped
1 (8-ounce) package cream cheese
1 teaspoon fresh mint, chiffonade

Pain Perdu The angel food cake should be at least a day old—the drier the better.

Combine all ingredients except cake and butter in a shallow dish. Dip two slices of cake into the mixture and only allow it to absorb enough liquid to just moisten the cake. Do not let it get soggy.

Melt 2 tablespoons butter in a large sauté pan. Place dipped slices of cake in pan and cook over medium heat until they are lightly browned on both sides. Remove and place on a buttered sheet pan. Repeat for remaining slices of cake and butter.

Bake pain perdu at 400 degrees F for 3–5 minutes. This will cause the pain perdu to puff slightly and cook thoroughly.

Hart Crane Peppermint Sauce Bring the butter, sugar, and cream to a moderate boil in a medium-sized saucepan and then remove from heat. Stir in the crushed peppermints, vanilla, and chocolate. Cover with plastic wrap and allow mixture to rest 2 minutes.

Remove the plastic wrap and whip with cream cheese until blended and creamy. Pour over pain perdu, garnish with mint chiffonade, and serve.

SUMMER AND SMOKE

B.L.T. Salad

serves 4 to 6

1 pound apple-smoked bacon,
cut into lardons
1 tablespoon Dijon mustard
2 teaspoons minced garlic
1 teaspoon chopped rosemary
$\frac{1}{2}$ teaspoon chopped tarragon
1$\frac{1}{2}$ teaspoons Worcestershire
sauce
1 teaspoon soy sauce
1 teaspoon prepared horseradish
1 cup olive oil
2 tablespoons mayonnaise
24 ounces mixed greens
3 Creole tomatoes, sliced
4–6 hard-boiled eggs, sliced into
quarters

In a medium sauté pan over medium heat, cook the bacon until almost crispy. Reserve $\frac{1}{4}$ cup of the bacon drippings. Drain bacon on a paper towel.

In a small bowl, combine the mustard, garlic, rosemary, tarragon, Worcestershire, soy sauce, horseradish, and olive oil. Fold in the mayonnaise.

In a medium-sized mixing bowl, gently toss the greens with the dressing. Divide the greens equally between plates and alternate tomatoes and egg quarters around the edge of each plate. Sprinkle with the cooked bacon. Drizzle a little of the warm reserved bacon fat over each plate before serving.

Cold "Cucumber Sandwich" Soup

serves 6 to 8

12 tablespoons unsalted butter, divided
6 slices white bread, crust removed, cubed
1 large onion, minced
6 large cucumbers, peeled, seeded, and chopped
1/2 loaf stale French bread, crust removed, broken
8 cups chicken stock
3 tablespoons chopped fresh dill, divided
Salt and pepper
4 cups heavy cream
1 teaspoon Tabasco or Crystal hot sauce
1/2 lemon, juiced
1 cucumber, finely diced
6–8 ounces Toffika or Bowfin caviar

Melt 6 tablespoons butter in a saucepan and set aside.

In an oven preheated to 400 degrees F, brown the cubed bread for 3–4 minutes. Remove from oven and then toss evenly in the melted butter. Return to the oven to toast for an additional 2 minutes.

Sauté the onion over low heat in the remaining butter for 3 minutes or until soft. Do not brown. Add the cucumber, French bread, stock, 2 tablespoons dill, and salt and pepper to taste. Cook for an additional 7 minutes. Remove from heat and let cool slightly. Puree and strain through a fine mesh strainer. Cool to room temperature then whisk in the cream, Tabasco, lemon juice, and 1 cucumber finely diced. Refrigerate for 2–3 hours.

You will have to hand whip the soup before serving to re-emulsify. Serve chilled and sprinkled with the remaining dill, caviar, and toasted bread cubes.

CHEF to cook

Perfect for Alma's Literary Symposium Brunch

Brussels Sprouts with Honey, Peaches, and Creole Mustard

serves 6

36 Brussels sprouts, rinsed and cleaned
8 tablespoons unsalted butter, divided
1 (12-ounce) can chicken stock
1 cup honey
1 tablespoon minced garlic
1 tablespoon lite soy sauce
1 teaspoon ground ginger
Salt and pepper
2 large peaches, peeled and cut in large dice
2 tablespoons Creole mustard

Sauté the Brussels sprouts in 4 tablespoons butter for 1 minute. Add the stock, honey, garlic, soy sauce, ginger, and salt and pepper to taste. Cover the pot with a heavy lid and let cook about 5–8 minutes or until tender.

Remove lid and add the remaining butter, peaches, and mustard. Reduce the juices by half to form a glaze and serve.

Haricots Verts with Dried Red Pepper, Lemon Glaze, Sliced Red Onion, and Sun-Dried Cherries

serves 6 to 8

2 cups water, divided
2 tablespoons sugar
1 lemon, zested, juice reserved
2 pounds baby green beans
1 cup sun-dried cherries
½ red onion, thinly sliced
1 cup extra virgin olive oil
1 teaspoon red pepper flakes
4 cloves garlic, sliced thinly lengthwise
Salt and pepper to taste

In a small saucepan, bring 1 cup of water and the sugar to a boil. Add the lemon zest and then remove from the heat. Let rest for 1 hour and then remove the zest with a fork or tongs.

In a sauté pan, place the green beans, cherries, and onion in 1 cup water with the olive oil and red pepper flakes. Bring to a boil, cover, and cook for 2 minutes or until beans are halfway cooked. Remove the cover and add the lemon juice and garlic. Sauté until beans are tender, about 8–10 minutes; the liquid will be reduced.

Transfer to a serving plate and toss in the fresh lemon juice. Season with the salt and pepper. Serve hot or at room temperature.

Louisiana Frog Legs with Orange-Tabasco Glaze

serves 6

ORANGE TABASCO GLAZE
1 cup water
1/2 cup sugar
2 cups orange juice
1 orange, zested
1 teaspoon ground ginger
1/2 teaspoon 5-spice powder
2 teaspoons soy sauce
1–2 tablespoons Tabasco

LOUISIANA FROG LEGS
2 eggs
12 Louisiana frog legs (chicken drummettes may be substituted)
Salt and pepper
All-purpose flour
Breadcrumbs
Peanut or canola oil for frying

Tabasco Glaze In a saucepan combine the water, sugar, orange juice, and zest; simmer over low heat for 30 minutes or until the zest is tender. Add the ginger, 5-spice powder, and soy sauce and reduce by half. Remove from heat and add the Tabasco.

Louisiana Frog Legs In a shallow bowl, mix eggs with a little water to make an egg wash. Season the legs with salt and pepper and then toss in the flour, dip in the egg wash, and then dredge in the breadcrumbs.

Heat oil in a skillet or fryer to 375 degrees F. Deep-fry or fry in hot oil for about 3–5 minutes or until golden. Do not overcook the legs as they will become tough. (In the event you have substituted chicken, make sure they are cooked thoroughly.) Carefully remove legs from oil and drain the excess oil onto paper towels.

To Serve Place the legs in a bowl and toss with the reduced sauce and serve.

Alma's Ambrosia "Fruit Punch" with Claret Southern-Style Fruit Salad

"I JUST DOTE ON CLARET."

serves 6

2 peaches, peeled and cubed
2 navel oranges, peeled and segmented
2 Granny Smith apples, peeled, cored, and cubed
1 large pineapple, peeled, cored, and cubed
1 pound red seedless grapes
3 red plums, pitted and cubed
1 pint blueberries or strawberries
2 bananas, peeled and cubed
1/2 cup shredded coconut
1 cup sugar, divided
1 1/2 cups water
2 cups sun-dried cherries
1 vanilla bean, split and scraped
1 cinnamon stick
8 ounces claret

Place the fruit with any juices and the coconut in a nonreactive bowl and toss in half of the sugar; set aside.

Heat the water in a pot with the vanilla, cinnamon, and the remaining sugar for 5 minutes or until you can smell the cinnamon. Pour over the cherries, cover, and let the cherries rehydrate.

When the cherries have reached room temperature, pour them (with the liquid) in with the fruit, add the claret and toss. Serve chilled.

Grilled Pork Tender Medallions, Yam Croûte and Pepper Jelly

serves 6

4 medium yams
Salt and pepper
2 red bell peppers, medium diced
2 green bell peppers,
medium diced
½ cup applejack brandy
1 cup orange juice
1½ cups light corn syrup
1 (12-ounce) pork tender, sliced
into 12 medallions
3 tablespoons Creole mustard

Wash the yams and then lightly coat in salt. Wrap in aluminum foil and bake at 450 degrees F for 20 minutes or until tender. Carefully remove yams from the foil and slice into 12 medallions, approximately 2 inches thick each. Flash fry or sauté the yam medallions until crispy.

In a large saucepan, combine the peppers, brandy, orange juice, and corn syrup over medium heat. Cook for 30 minutes until the peppers have reduced in size by half and the mixture has thickened and reduced by one-third; let cool. (This jelly will keep in a refrigerator for 1–2 weeks.) For this recipe, serve the jelly at room temperature.

Season the pork medallions with salt, pepper, and mustard and grill for 2 minutes on each side until medium-rare. As an alternative, the tenders can be seasoned and grilled whole and sliced just prior to serving.

Place a dollop of the pepper jelly on top of a yam croûte and place a pork medallion on top of that. Drizzle a little more jelly onto the pork and serve.

Chocolate and Strawberry Bombe, Baked-Alaska Style

serves 6

1 pint high-quality vanilla
ice cream
2 pints high-quality dark chocolate
ice cream
2 pints high-quality strawberry
ice cream
Cooking oil
4 ounces strawberries, diced
½ cup sugar
1 teaspoon chopped fresh mint
8 ounces dark chocolate, shaved
3–4 slices pound cake or génoise
meringue
Basic Meringue (see below)

BASIC MERINGUE (SWISS STYLE)
2 cups sugar
⅔ cup water
8 egg whites
1 tablespoon vanilla extract
(even though Alma's
mom didn't want vanilla)

Remove the ice cream from the freezer and let soften (not melt) so that it can be reformed. Spray cooking oil onto a 4-quart stainless steel bowl. Line bowl with plastic wrap using one large piece extending well over the rim.

Mix the strawberries with the sugar and mint and let sit for 15–20 minutes until the berries macerate. Remove the berries and drain, reserving liquid.

In a small saucepan over medium heat, reduce the reserved syrup and then let cool.

Line inside of the stainless steel bowl's bottom and sides with the chocolate ice cream on one side and strawberry ice cream on the other, leaving a 2-cup-sized space or indentation in the center.

Blend the vanilla ice cream with the berries and the shaved chocolate and fill the space between the ice creams. Top the ice cream with slices of the cake and press down into the ice cream. Cover with the extended plastic wrap and freeze overnight for at least 12 hours.

Basic Meringue Bring the sugar and water to a boil for 3–6 minutes. Dip your forefinger and thumb in ice cold water and then very briefly dip the tips of your fingers into the syrup to get a small amount on your fingertips. Move your fingers back and forth and away from each other and a string should form. If not, cook mixture a little longer and test again. (This takes a little practice).

Beat the egg whites on high until semi-stiff and add the vanilla. Pour the hot syrup in a steady stream into the mixer while on high speed and beat until stiff and shiny. Allow to cool slightly. Transfer to a pastry bag for the "bomb" or use to top pies, cakes, and other desserts.

When Ready to Serve Remove the "bombe" from the freezer and carefully dip the bowl into a large pot of boiling water for 30 seconds. On a large heatproof plate, invert the "bombe." Using a pastry bag, pipe meringue to cover the "bombe" and use a cook's propane kitchen torch to brown it. Slice with a hot knife and serve.

CHEF to cook

Great for times of hysterical requests.

FOOD AND CLASS

Until recent decades, Southerners tended to assign certain foods and drinks to certain social classes; these days, many of those déclassé foods have become standard parts of menus in expensive restaurants. That class distinction is evident in several of the plays of Tennessee Williams. For example, drinking beer from a bucket is an act that automatically condemns one to the status of the untouchable. In the early *Battle of Angels*, Blanch sarcastically insists that Dolly's father in Blue Mountain "sits on the porch with his shoes off drinkin' beer out of a bucket!" and in *The Rose Tattoo*, Alvaro complains that his "dependents" do nothing but play Parcheesi and pass "a bucket of beer around the table." The distinction between the backgrounds of Stanley Kowalski and the DuBois sisters in *Streetcar* is clearly indicated in the comment that Stanley takes the last pork chop and "eats with his fingers." Maggie, pointing out to her husband Brick how her family is superior to that of Sister Woman's, criticizes her sister-in-law's children, as in the opening line of *Cat on a*

Hot Tin Roof: "One of those no-neck monsters hit me with a hot buttered biscuit so I have t'change!" The conversation between Myrtle and Chicken in *Kingdom of Earth* speaks volumes about food and class distinctions; when Chicken is frying bacon and potatoes together, Myrtle comes to the kitchen because "I thought I smelt French fries down here," to which Chicken replies, " There's potatoes down here but there's nothing French about it." A discussion about junk food in *Small Craft Warnings* touches on the question of class and food. When Violet asks Steve to get her "a hot dog with chili and onions . . . ," Leone retorts, "I heard on TV that the Food Administration found insect and rodent parts in some hot dogs sold lately." Later, Violet requests a Whopper from "King Burger," and Steve insists that "Being a cook I know the quality of those giant hamburgers called Whoppers, and they're fit only for dogfood."

A major milestone in the life of young Tom Williams occurred when he was seventeen and was briefly freed from the annoyance of St. Louis life when he joined a group of parishioners the Rev. Walter Dakins led on a trip to Europe. On 13 July 1928, the teenager wrote to his family from the liner *Homeric* that his grandfather "keeps his tongue pretty slick with Manhattan cocktails and Rye-Ginger Ales. I have tried them all but prefer none to plain ginger ale and Coca-Cola." However, he wrote to Edwina a week later that on their first evening in Paris, he drank "a whole glass of French champagne and am feeling consequently very elated . . . French champagne is the only drink that I like here." In later years, his preferred drinks were Jack Daniels and Martinis and the Italian wine Valpolicella.

One would imagine that after the traumatic move to St. Louis, the Williams family ate much the same as they had in Mississippi, and two plays dealing with life in that city, which Tennessee referred to as "St. Pollution," contain numerous references to food and drink. If we take *The Glass Menagerie* to reflect the reality of life in the Williams household, life must have been painful for the budding playwright. In the first scene, Amanda Wingfield, modeled on Edwina Williams, makes mealtime an ordeal for her son Tom: "Honey, don't *push* with your *fingers.* If you have to push with something, the thing to push with is a crust of bread. And chew—chew! Animals have secretions in their stomachs which enable them to digest food without mastication; but human beings are supposed to chew their food before they swallow it down. Eat food leisurely, son, and really enjoy it. A well-cooked meal has lots of delicate flavors that have to be held in the mouth for appreciation. So chew your food and give your salivary glands a chance to function!" A disgusted Tom responds, "I haven't enjoyed one bite of this dinner because of your constant directions on how to eat it. It's you that make me rush through meals with your hawk-like attention to every bite I take. Sickening—spoils my appetite—all this discussion of—animals' secretions—salivary glands—mastication!" Tom, often hungover from the excesses of the night before, is grilled by his suspicious mother at breakfast: "Eat a bowl of Purina! Shredded wheat biscuit?"

In *A Lovely Sunday for Creve Coeur,* set in St. Louis at a later time, Tennessee seems almost to be satirizing the eating habits of the "large midwestern city," as he terms it. Much of the play concerns the clash between the descendants of German settlers of the city and people who consider themselves superior to the immigrant population. In the opening scene Bodey is preparing

WHICH CAME FIRST FRIED CHICKEN OR DEVILED EGGS?

BODEY, WHO IS HARD OF HEARING, REPLIES:

"THIS IS THE BEST SUNDAY YET FOR A PICNIC AT CREVE COEUR."

fried chicken and deviled eggs for a picnic at Creve Coeur park. When her apartment mate Dorothea, who aspires to move up in the world, sardonically inquires, "Which came first, fried chicken or deviled eggs?" Bodey, who is hard of hearing, replies, "This is the best Sunday yet for a picnic at Creve Coeur." Later, Dorothea protests that if Bodey had her way, "my life would be just one long Creve Coeur interspersed with knockwurst, sauerkraut-hot potato salad dinners . . . ." Further humor at the expense of the St. Louis Germans occurs in the phone call from Buddy to his sister Bodey to complain that she has kept him waiting so long he has drunk "two beers and made a liverwurst sandwich . . . ." In an exchange that underscores the differences in ethnic groups in the city, Bodey greets Sophie Gluck, an upstairs neighbor, who "comes down for a coffee and cruller at ten," Helena, who teaches with Dorothea and wants her to move from Bodey's and share an apartment with her, inquires, "What is a cruller?" Bodey: "Aw. You call it a doughnut, but me, bein' German, was raised to call it a cruller." Helena: "Oh. A cruller is a doughnut but you call it a cruller . . . I don't care for the cruller, as you call it. Pastries are not included in my diet."

The fact that Tennessee Williams was so turned off by St. Louis—and particularly its cuisine—may account for *A Lovely Sunday for Creve Coeur*'s being one of his lesser known plays.

It was at the University of Missouri and then at the University of Iowa that the dramatist's eating and drinking habits seem to have changed. In April of 1932, he wrote to his mother from Columbia, Missouri, "We had a real banquet this noon, caviar in anchovy paste, spring chicken, and strawberry short cake." His taste for alcohol is demonstrated in a letter he wrote from St. Louis to Clark Mills in September of 1937, in which he writes that he, William Jay Smith, and others read and critiqued Smith's poetry and "drank great quantities of beer. . . . I want you to know that I have already purchased a pint of good whiskey to fortify myself against the rigors of a northern winter." The last remark relates to his preparations to go to the University of Iowa to pursue his education, and having been to Iowa, I would suggest that one pint is not enough!

Tennessee Williams at Ocho Rios, Jamaica, 1962

Soon the "northern winters" would be behind him, for he returned to the Deep South in December 1938 when he went to New Orleans for the first time and settled briefly in the French Quarter. After the deprivations of college life, a consequence of his father's penury, Tennessee was delighted to find in the Southern city an abundance of great food at low prices. "Food is amazingly cheap," he wrote to Edwina on 2 January 1939. "I get breakfast at the French Market for a dime. Lunch and dinner amount to about forty cents at a good cafeteria near Canal Street. And the cooking is the best I've encountered away from home [Notice that qualifying phrase, "away from home," lest Miss Edwina's feelings be hurt.] Raw oysters, twenty cents a dozen! Shrimp, crab, lobster, and all kinds of fish—I have a passion for sea-food which makes their abundance a great joy." When the landlady of his boarding house on Toulouse Street opened a lunch room, for which he served as promoter, waiter, cashier, and dishwasher, he wrote that Mrs. Anderson's "cooking is the best I've ever tasted," forgetting his concern for Miss Edwina's feelings in his enthusiasm.

In the plays that Tennessee wrote about those early stays in New Orleans, he celebrates the food of the Creole city with gusto. The autobiographical *Vieux Carre*, 1977, contains perhaps the most references to food of any of Williams's works, I suspect because in those early French Quarter days, the struggling writer must have gone hungry on more than one occasion. Two characters in that play are elderly ladies, down on their luck, who retrieve food from garbage cans in the French Quarter and return with it to the boarding house at 722 Toulouse Street, where Tom Williams lived in early 1939. Their actions and remarks reveal much about the faded grandeur that the playwright witnessed among residents of the region at that time of Depression.

Mary Maude: Miss Carrie and I ordered a little more dinner this evening than we could eat, so we had the waiter put the remains of the . . . .

Miss Carrie: The steak "Diane," I had the steak Diane and Mary Maude had the chicken "bonne femme." But our eyes were a little bigger than our stomachs.

Mary Maude: The sight of too much food on a table can kill your appetite! But the food is too good to waste.

Mrs. Wire, the landlady, is deliberately cruel to the elderly tenants, taunting them with the protective lies they tell, and late one night when she is cooking a gumbo, the two come to the kitchen in the hope of being fed. "I suddenly get a notion to cook a gumbo," Mrs. Wire says, "and when I do the smell of it is an attraction, draws company to the kitchen." The landlady offers her tenants some but first pretends to spit in it, saying, "I always spit in a pot of gumbo to give it special flavor, like a bootblack spits on a shoe." When Miss Carrie and Mary Maude say that they "are compiling a cookbook which we hope to have published. A Creole cookbook, recipes we remember from our childhood," Mrs. Wire replies cruelly, "A recipe is a poor substitute for food." Jane, another tenant, is so moved by the plight of the two elderly ladies that she asks Nursie, the maid, if their pride would be offended if she "bought them a sack of groceries at Solari's tomorrow"–Solari's being a legendary grocery store and delicatessen in the French Quarter that Tennessee frequented—to which Nursie replies, "Honey, they gone as far past pride as they gone past mistaking a buzzard for a blackbird."

In his correspondence from the late 1930s, Tennessee Williams reveals repeatedly his love of the venerable old restaurants in New Orleans, particularly Galatoire's, where, he wrote to Miss Edwina, he had amazingly inexpensive and delicious seafood meals. In *Vieux Carre* the character of the artist, Nightingale, provides an almost Whitmanesque catalogue of the famous dining establishments of the time in the city. He begins by a condemnation of "the Two Parrots," based on the Court of Two Sisters, where Tennessee was briefly a waiter, at which, Nightingale insists, "the menu sometimes includes cockroaches," and continues to list "the great eating places." Finally, Mrs. Wire decides to open a restaurant in her rooming house because compared to her, there is "no better cooking in the Garden District or the Vieux Carre." In the short play *The Mutilated*, Celeste and Trinket have a typical New Orleans conversation about food, discussing Chinese food in the Quarter, and Commander's Palace; tomorrow, Celeste says, "we'll have lunch together at Arnaud's. Oysters Rockefeller? . . . Then a shrimp bisque. . . ." Until his death, Galatoire's continued to be Tennessee's favorite New Orleans eatery, which explains his use of it in several plays, most notably *Streetcar*, in which Stella announces to Stanley on his poker night that she is "taking

Baby Doll (1956)
Directed by Elia Kazan
Shown on poster: Carroll
Baker (as Baby Doll
Meighan), Eli Wallach,
Karl Malden

Blanche to Galatoire's for supper." Alas, we do not know what the two Delta ladies ordered at the bistro, but I judge Blanche to be the Trout Amandine type. (In those days, they would have had drinks served over hand-chipped ice, which, sad to say, has been replaced, thanks to the monster known as "Progress.")

In those early years in the French Quarter, Tennessee took note of the street vendors who sold vegetables, hot tamales, pralines, and other items, and these turn up in several of the plays. The acting version of *Streetcar* opens with a tamale vendor chanting, chorus-like, "Red hots! Red hots!" Later Blanche observes that "Even the hot tamale man has deserted the street, and he hangs on till the end." The mythical town in which *Camino Real* is set is, the playwright says, based on several real places, including New Orleans. Early in the play a peddler enters chanting, "Tacos, tacos, fritos," and later they advertise "Dulces, dulces! . . . Pasteles, café con leche!" [Sweets, sweets! . . . Pastries, coffee with milk!]

Tennessee began most mornings in those early years with coffee at the Morning Call, a French Quarter institution, the best of the French Market coffee stands, which is, alas, no more. This surely provided the impetus for such a passage as that in *Vieux Carre* in which Nursie asks Jane to "have some hot chick'ry with me?" Jane, a New Yorker, replies, "Do you know, I still don't know what chickory is?" and Nursie explains, "Why, chickory's South'n style coffee."

Other New Orleans touches in Tennessee's plays include references to po' boy sandwiches and several local bars: Dixie's Bar of Music, the Twilight Lounge, and a neighbor of Kowalskis warns a sailor going into the Four Deuces in the opening scene, "Don't let them sell you a Blue Moon cocktail or you won't go out on your own feet."

ELIA KAZAN'S
PRODUCTION OF
TENNESSEE WILLIAMS'
BOLDEST STORY!

...this is

baby doll

She's nineteen.

She makes her husband keep away

Her name is
CARROLL BAKER!
Her role is
raw electricity!
Her portrayal
is a sensation!

VIEUX CARRE

Chicken Bonne Femme

serves 6

6 chicken breasts
1½ cups peanut oil
Salt and pepper
1 cup all-purpose flour
1 large onion, sliced
1 cup dry white wine
4 cups chicken stock
1 tablespoon Worcestershire sauce
10 cloves garlic, thinly sliced
3 large russet potatoes, peeled and cut in 1-inch cubes
½ cup chopped Italian flat-leaf parsley
1 pound thick-sliced ham, cut in 1-inch cubes
2 tablespoons unsalted butter

Season chicken with salt and pepper. In a large frying pan with a little peanut oil, sear the breasts. Remove the breasts and dredge in flour seasoned with salt and pepper. Add remaining oil to the pan and, when hot, sauté the breasts on both sides. Remove from pan and discard two-thirds of the oil.

Add onion to the pan and sauté over medium heat for 3–4 minutes. Return the chicken to the pan, deglaze with the wine, and reduce the liquid by two-thirds. Add the chicken stock, Worcestershire, garlic, potatoes, and parsley and simmer for about 40 minutes or until the potatoes are tender.

In a separate skillet, sauté the ham in butter over medium heat until the ham is a light brown color on all sides. Once the potatoes are thoroughly tender, add the ham with the butter into the pot with the chicken and then serve.

Lavender, Honey, and Goat Cheese Beignets with Metaxa Brandy and Orange Drizzle

serves 6

CHEESE BALLS
1 pound chèvre (goat cheese)
1 teaspoon honey
¼ teaspoon dried lavender flowers
¼ cup confectioners' sugar

ORANGE DRIZZLE
1 cup fresh orange juice
1 cup sugar
1 tablespoon orange zest
2 cups water
1 cup Metaxa brandy

BEIGNETS
2 cups all-purpose flour
2 eggs
½ cup sugar
1 tablespoon baking powder
Pinch kosher salt
1 teaspoon pure vanilla extract
3 cups half-and-half
8 cups peanut oil

Cheese Balls In a blender, combine the cheese, honey, lavender, and confectioners' sugar and blend very well. Roll into ½-inch balls and freeze overnight or for at least 2 hours.

Orange Drizzle Combine the orange juice, sugar, orange zest, and water in a sauté pan and cook over high heat for 10 minutes, reducing by half. Add the brandy; remove from heat and let cool slightly.

Beignets Combine the flour, eggs, sugar, baking powder, salt, vanilla, and half-and-half in a bowl.

Heat the oil in a fryer to 375 degrees F. Dip the frozen cheese balls into the batter and carefully place into the fryer a few at a time. Fry for about 1–2 minutes or until golden brown. Remove and place on paper towels to drain.

To Serve Dust beignets with confectioners' sugar, arrange on a plate, and drizzle with the orange glaze.

Creole-Style Chicken, Andouille, and Okra Gumbo

serves 10 to 12

STOCK

2 whole chickens, roasted
(store-bought is fine)
4 quarts water
4 ribs celery, chopped
3 large onions, chopped
4 large carrots, chopped

GUMBO

2 pounds andouille sausage
1/2 cup butter
1/2 cup peanut oil
1 cup all-purpose flour
4 ribs celery, chopped
4 large onions, chopped
2 large bell peppers, chopped
6 cloves garlic, minced
10 sprigs thyme or 1 tablespoon
dried thyme
1/4 tablespoon dried lavender
flowers
3–4 tablespoons Worcestershire
sauce
2 tablespoons soy sauce
Creole seasoning
Salt and pepper
2 pounds okra, cut into rounds
Steamed rice

Stock Debone the roasted chickens (reserve chicken meat), discard the skin, and add the chicken bones to a large stockpot with the 4 quarts of water. Add the celery, onions, and carrots and cook for 6 hours over very low heat (155 degrees F). Strain the stock into another pot and set aside. Discard the vegetables and chicken bones.

Gumbo Cook the sausage in an oven until it is two-thirds cooked; drain excess oil, dice sausage, and set aside. In a heavy-bottomed skillet, melt the butter and then add the oil and flour until it reaches a smooth consistency. Stir constantly over low to medium heat to make a roux. Cook the roux extremely carefully until it reaches a dark caramel color for a nutty taste.

Add the mirepoix of vegetables to the roux in the skillet, stir periodically, and cook for 7–10 minutes. Put this mixture into the empty gumbo pot.

Over low heat, slowly add the fresh stock to the roux with the mirepoix and whisk to ensure smoothness. Add the Worcestershire, soy sauce, and

continue on page 62

seasonings and cook for 4–6 hours over low heat, stirring periodically.

When gumbo is cooked, add the sausage, reserved chicken meat, and okra and cook an additional 15 minutes.

To Serve Spoon gumbo over steamed rice. Freeze the leftovers.

CHEF to cook

There are so many variations of this dish, I simply want to give you the necessary road map and tips to ensure success. A gumbo should always start with a fresh stock. This is a dish that should not be rushed. You should also note that the proteins were not added until the gumbo was basically cooked. Adding proteins early, especially seafood, will not enhance the flavor, but will instead cause the gumbo to lose texture and integrity.

GUMBO

ORIGINATED IN THE 18TH CENTURY
COMBINING INGREDIENTS
FROM THE FRENCH, SPANISH, WEST
AFRICAN, AND CHOCTAW CULTURES.

"A TRUE ART FORM"

A STAPLE & TRIBUTE
TO THE GOOD FOLKS OF NEW ORLEANS

Gumbo Po' Boy with Chicken, Andouille, and Okra

"A RECIPE IS A POOR SUBSTITUTE FOR FOOD."

serves 6

6 (8-inch) loaves French bread, sliced lengthwise
Creole-Style Chicken, Andouille, and Okra Gumbo (page 60)
½ cup butter
Romaine lettuce, chiffonade
Pickles, sliced
1 Creole tomato, sliced
1 cup good-quality mayonnaise

Take the bottom half of the sliced French bread and remove some of the white bread inside to create a "boat." Repeat for each loaf. Butter and then toast both halves in the oven for 2 minutes.

Heat gumbo and then, using a slotted spoon, fill the bread with meat and okra. Try not to add too much of the juice or the po' boy will become too sloppy.

Dress the sandwiches with the lettuce, pickles, and tomatoes tossed lightly in mayonnaise and serve.

CHEF to cook

This is a great use of gumbo leftovers and a reinvention of a classic New Orleans sandwich.

Chicory Coffee with White Port Wine, Blue Cheese, and Blueberry Vinaigrette Served on a "Cold Biscuit" Crouton

serves 6 to 8

VINAIGRETTE

1 pint blueberries, divided
1 cup port
1/2 cup balsamic vinegar
1/2 cup Community-brand chicory coffee
2 teaspoons sugar
1 tablespoon Worcestershire sauce
1 clove garlic, sliced
1 tablespoon Creole or grainy mustard
1–2 cups extra virgin olive oil
1/2 onion, thinly sliced
Salt and pepper

SALAD AND BISCUITS

4 tablespoons unsalted butter
3 biscuits, baked and sliced in half
1 large head frisée, washed and thoroughly dried
8 ounces blue cheese
1/2 red onion, thinly sliced

Vinaigrette In a saucepan, place half of the blueberries, port, vinegar, coffee, sugar, Worcestershire, and garlic and cook over high heat for 10 minutes, stirring lightly. Remove from heat and allow to cool slightly. Puree in a blender, strain, and cool completely.

Place puree in a stainless steel bowl. Add mustard. Slowly add oil while blending to emulsify. Add the onion and salt and pepper to taste. Let rest for 2 minutes.

Salad and Biscuits Heat butter in a sauté pan and toast the biscuit slices until both sides are lightly browned and crispy. Arrange the biscuits on plates. Break up and toss the frisée with the vinaigrette and then place some dressed salad on top of each biscuit slice. Arrange the remaining blueberries, blue cheese, and onions around the salad and drizzle with additional vinaigrette. Serve.

CHEF to cook

Coffee should be brewed.

Tenderloin of Pork "Steak Diane" and Lyonnaise Potatoes with Rosemary and Haricots Verts with Red Pepper and Lemon Zest

serves 6

TENDERLOIN OF PORK "STEAK DIANE"

2 whole pork tenders
(7 ounces each)
Salt and pepper
3 tablespoons brandy
2 tablespoons peanut or olive oil
3 tablespoons capers, drained
1 tablespoon finely minced garlic
2 tablespoons Dijon mustard
1 tablespoon chopped parsley
1 teaspoon freshly squeezed
lemon juice
1 teaspoon Worcestershire sauce
1½ cups veal demi-glace*

LYONNAISE POTATOES WITH ROSEMARY

1 medium onion, sliced
6 tablespoons butter, divided
2 cups chicken stock
2 cloves minced garlic
5 potatoes, peeled and cut into
1-inch-thick slices
1 teaspoon soy sauce
2 teaspoons Worcestershire sauce
Salt and freshly ground pepper
½ to 1 tablespoon chopped fresh
rosemary

*This is available in specialty stores

Tenderloin of Pork "Steak Diane" Cut the pork into 18 (1½-inch) medallions and season with salt and pepper. In a very hot skillet, sear both sides of the meat until brown, about 1 minute per side. Deglaze with the brandy and then remove meat and place on a plate.

Reduce the heat under the skillet to medium. Add remaining ingredients and simmer for 2–3 minutes until the sauce slightly thickens. Return the pork to the sauce and cook an additional 4 minutes, until the pork is medium rare to medium. Serve on a plate with the Lyonnaise Potatoes and the Haricot Verts.

Lyonnaise Potatoes with Rosemary Sauté the onion in half of the butter over medium heat until translucent and slightly browned. Add the stock, garlic, potatoes, soy sauce, Worcestershire, salt, and pepper and cook over low heat, covered, for 15–20 minutes, or until the potatoes are two-thirds done. Add the remaining butter and rosemary and cook, uncovered, over medium to high heat until the potatoes are lightly browned. Serve.

HARICOTS VERTS WITH RED PEPPER AND LEMON ZEST

2 pounds fresh haricots verts
1 tablespoon unsalted butter
1 teaspoon lemon zest
1/4 teaspoon crushed and dried red pepper flakes
Salt and pepper
1 teaspoon fresh lemon juice

Haricots Verts with Red Pepper and Lemon Zest Blanch the trimmed green beans in boiling, salted water for 1–2 minutes, or until slightly tender but firm.

In sauté pan, melt the butter and then add the zest and pepper flakes and let simmer over low heat for 1 minute. Add the blanched beans and adjust seasoning with salt and pepper. Remove beans from the pan to a serving bowl and toss with the lemon juice. Serve.

Oysters en Brochette

serves 6

12 slices good-quality bacon
12 Louisiana Gulf oysters (2 per person)
Salt and pepper
Toothpicks
2 tablespoons Worcestershire sauce
1 large lemon, juiced
2 tablespoons chopped parsley

Broil the bacon in the oven on a sheet pan until halfway cooked. Let cool slightly and then remove bacon, reserving the pan with drippings to finish the dish.

Season the oysters with salt and pepper. Wrap 2 oysters each with a strip of bacon and secure with toothpicks. Return to sheet pan. Place pan in the oven and bake at 450 degrees F for 3–5 minutes. When the oysters have begun to curl and the bacon has finished cooking, sprinkle evenly with the Worcestershire, lemon juice, and parsley; broil for 2 minutes. Serve immediately.

Trout-Pecan Meunière with Bacon and Yukon Gold Potatoes Sautéed with Sugar Snap Peas

serves 6

TROUT-PECAN MEUNIÈRE

6 trout fillets (5 ounces each)
Salt and pepper
1/2 cup all-purpose flour, seasoned
2 tablespoons peanut oil
1/2 cup red wine
1 cup chicken stock
1 cup veal demi-glace*
2 tablespoons Worcestershire sauce
2 teaspoons minced garlic
2 tablespoons chopped Italian flat-leaf parsley, divided
4 scallions, white and green separated and sliced
1 teaspoon Creole mustard
2 cups pecan halves
8 tablespoons unsalted butter
1 lemon, juiced

This is available in specialty stores

Trout-Pecan Meunière Season the fish with salt and pepper. Dredge in the flour and knock off excess flour. Pour the oil into a sauté pan and heat over medium heat. Place fillets top side down and sauté for 1–2 minutes on each side or until very lightly colored. Remove from pan. Carefully pour off excess oil and return pan to heat and deglaze with the wine. Add the stock, demi-glace, Worcestershire, garlic, half of the parsley, the white tips of the scallions, and mustard. Simmer on high heat for 2 minutes to bring the flavors together.

Return fish to the pan and simmer for 2 minutes on each side. Remove fish to plates. Add the pecans and remaining ingredients to sauté pan; stir sauce together for 1–2 minutes.

Pour the sauce over each of the fillets and serve with Bacon and Yukon Gold Potatoes.

CHEF to cook

This is an old New Orleans restaurant staple with a twist.

BACON AND YUKON GOLD
POTATOES SAUTÉED
WITH SUGAR SNAP PEAS
3 large Yukon Gold potatoes,
cut in ½-inch slices
9 strips high-quality apple-
smoked bacon
Salt and pepper
3–4 cups chicken stock
36 sugar snap peas

Bacon and Yukon Gold Potatoes Sautéed with Sugar Snap Peas
Blanch the potato slices in boiling salted water until
half cooked; drain. Bake the bacon at 450 degrees F
until crispy, then remove bacon to paper towels and
drain and cool. Reserve bacon fat. Crumble bacon and
set aside.

Using a very large flat-bottomed sauté pan (large
enough that the potato slices will not touch very
much), add the reserved bacon fat to the pan with the
potatoes, salt and pepper, and 1 cup stock. Allow to
simmer, covered, for 3–4 minutes, flipping the potatoes occasionally. Add another cup of stock or more as
needed until the potatoes are cooked until tender, not
mushy. Add the peas and adjust seasoning with salt
and pepper. Serve with the crispy bacon bits sprinkled
over top.

CHEF to cook

This dish is derived from Tennessee
Williams's *Kingdom on Earth* and
is used here because it works well
with trout or any fish.

BATTLE
OF ANGELS
AND ORPHEUS
DESCENDING

Herb-Roasted New Potato Salad

serves 6

10–16 new potatoes, washed and cut into quarters
8 quarts salted water
1½ cups extra virgin olive oil
1 tablespoon chopped parsley
1 teaspoon chopped rosemary
2 teaspoons chopped thyme
1 teaspoon lemon zest
Salt and pepper to taste

DRESSING
1 cup mayonnaise
1 tablespoon honey
1 tablespoon Dijon mustard
1 tablespoon prepared horseradish
2 ribs celery, cut in diagonals
3 tablespoons Smoked Garlic Vinaigrette (page 131)
1 tablespoon chopped fresh parsley

In a large pot, start the potatoes in cold salted water and boil until potatoes are cooked. Drain well and add to a cast-iron skillet. Add a little olive oil, sauté, and cover potatoes with remaining oil and start browning. Add the herbs and lemon zest; toss well. Bake at 425 degrees F for about 15–20 minutes, stirring often. Check for doneness of the potatoes with a skewer and remove when potatoes are tender to their center. Allow to cool to room temperature and add the dressing. This dish can be served hot or cold.

Dressing Combine all ingredients well and then toss into the potatoes.

Olive Nut Sandwich with Two-Olive Tapenade, Toasted Pine Nuts, and Feta Cheese

serves 6

6 slices multigrain bread
4–6 tablespoons unsalted butter
1½ to 2 cups Two-Olive Tapenade
(see below)
1½ ounces feta cheese
1 cup pine nuts, toasted
1 cup finely chopped roma
tomatoes
2 teaspoons chopped Italian
flat-leaf parsley

TWO-OLIVE TAPENADE
(MAKES 2 CUPS)
4 cups ripe olives, pitted and
drained
1 cup kalamata olives with
juice, deseeded
2 teaspoons finely minced garlic
4 large basil leaves, finely minced
Salt and pepper
1½ cups extra virgin olive oil
2 tablespoons chopped parsley

Cut the bread into fourths (to make two little sandwiches per slice). Fry the bread in butter in a skillet until golden and toasted on both sides. Transfer to a sheet pan and allow to cool.

Two-Olive Tapenade Carefully pulse olives in a food processor until coarsely chopped. Stir in the garlic and basil. Adjust seasoning with salt and pepper. Add the olive oil. Pulse just to incorporate the oil into the olive mixture. Remove mixture from food processor and stir in parsley by hand.

To Serve Place about 1 tablespoon of the tapenade to generously cover the bottoms of half the pieces of the toast, about ¼-inch thick. Place 1 teaspoon of the cheese on top of the tapenade and then sprinkle with 1 teaspoon of the pine nuts. Top with the tomatoes as a garnish and place the other piece of toast on top. Repeat until all sandwiches are made. Sprinkle with the parsley and serve.

Breast of Chicken and Mushroom Risotto Croquettes with Bacon Leek Cream

serves 6

CROQUETTES

3 whole chicken breasts, cut into
¼-inch cubes
All-purpose flour, seasoned
3 tablespoons butter, divided
1 cup minced onion
1 cup minced bell pepper
2 teaspoons minced garlic
1 cup Marsala or Madeira
1½ cups sliced mushrooms
1½ cups chicken stock
1 tablespoon Worcestershire sauce
1 teaspoon chopped fresh thyme
2 tablespoons cream
2 cups cooked risotto
Salt and pepper
1 egg, whipped
1 cup grated Romano cheese

BACON LEEK CREAM
(MAKES 3 CUPS)

8 strips apple-smoked bacon
1½ cups Leek Confit (see below)
4 cups heavy cream
½ teaspoon nutmeg
1 tablespoon finely minced garlic
Salt and pepper

LEEK CONFIT

2 large leek bottoms,
white part only
2 tablespoons extra virgin olive oil

Croquettes Dust chicken in flour. Sauté chicken in 2 tablespoons butter until lightly browned on all sides. Add remaining butter, onion, bell pepper, and garlic and sauté for 2 minutes. Deglaze with the Marsala or Madeira, and then add the mushrooms. Add the stock, Worcestershire, and thyme and cook over medium-high heat until the mushrooms and chicken are just cooked, about 10 minutes. Remove chicken and vegetables from the sauté pot and reserve.

Add cream to the pan and cook over medium heat to reduce by one-third. Stir in the risotto. (The mixture should be smooth and thick.) Remove from heat and let cool to room temperature. Adjust seasoning with salt and pepper. Add the whipped egg and mix well. Add the Romano cheese. Divide evenly and form into 12 croquettes (football shapes). Refrigerate for 2–4 hours.

Bacon Leek Cream Cook the bacon until crispy; remove from pan and drain excess fat from the bacon onto paper towels. Reserve the bacon drippings. Add the Leek Confit to the drippings and stir. Add the cream, nutmeg, and garlic and cook over medium heat, reducing by one-third. The sauce should be thick.

Leek Confit Remove the green tops from the leeks and soak the white bottoms in clean water for 15 minutes. Remove from water and ensure that they are clean. Julienne the leeks and toss in the remaining

continued on page 76

1 cup white wine
4 large sprigs fresh thyme, chopped
Salt and pepper to taste

FOR FRYING
All-purpose flour
Egg wash
Ground semolina
Peanut oil or canola oil
Lemon wedge for serving

ingredients. Place in a roasting pan covered with foil. Bake for approximately 12 minutes in a preheated 350-degree-F oven until leeks are tender.

When Ready to Serve Dredge the croquettes in flour, dip in egg wash, and dust with ground semolina. Heat oil to 350 degrees F. Pan-fry or deep-fry croquettes, a few at a time, in the hot oil. Drain on paper towels. Serve with a lemon wedge. Or, for a country fried steak effect, serve topped with the Bacon Leek Cream with roasted potatoes and String Beans with Shiitake "Bacon" and Garlic (see facing page) on the side.

Avocado and Smoked Gouda Frittata with Wasabi Peas

serves 6

4 tablespoons butter
14 eggs, whipped with salt and pepper to taste
2 medium ripe avocados, pitted, peeled, and sliced 1/2-inch thick
1/2 lemon, juiced
1/2 pound smoked Gouda cheese, skin removed and julienned
1/2 pound fontina cheese, cut into 1/4-inch slices
2 cups wasabi peas, coarsely crushed

Heat an 8-inch ovenproof skillet and coat with non-stick spray. Add the butter. When the butter starts to sizzle, pour in two-thirds of the eggs. Let bottom of eggs set over medium-low heat.

Drizzle the avocado slices with the lemon juice. When the bottom of the eggs have set, arrange the slices of the avocado around the eggs. Add the Gouda and then the fontina cheese. Ladle the remaining eggs over top.

Place skillet in a 450-degree-F oven for 7–10 minutes or until puffy and cooked. Remove and let rest for 5 minutes. Slice and garnish with the crushed wasabi peas.

String Beans with Shiitake "Bacon" and Garlic

serves 6

STRING BEANS
5 large garlic cloves, peeled
Salt and pepper
3 tablespoons unsalted butter
1–2 pounds fresh baby string
beans, cleaned

SHIITAKE "BACON"
12 large shiitake mushrooms
6 cups peanut oil

String Beans Place the garlic and a pinch of salt in a small saucepan and cover with water. Bring to a boil, remove from heat, drain, and let cool. When the garlic is cool enough to handle, slice very thinly, about $1/8$ inch thick, and let drain on a paper towel.

Heat a 10-quart pot of salted water to the boiling point. In a sauté pan, melt the butter and add the garlic slices; sauté over medium heat until the garlic turns light brown. Blanch the beans in boiling water for 2 minutes before adding them to the garlic and butter. Adjust seasonings with salt and pepper, toss, and cook for 1 minute. Beans should be al dente. Plate and serve with the Shiitake Bacon sprinkled on top.

Shiitake "Bacon" Slice the mushrooms paper-thin, $1/16$ inch or thinner if you can. The trick for this dish is to endeavor to make the cuts as uniform as possible to achieve the proper result.

Heat the fresh peanut oil to 375 degrees F in a deep fryer or pot and carefully drop in the mushrooms. Let fry over high heat until no bubbles are present. Carefully remove and drain on a paper towel. Season lightly with salt and pepper.

Sautéed Ham and Turnip Greens with NOLA Brewing Irish Channel Stout Beer

serves 6

½ pound apple-smoked bacon
1 medium-sized onion, chopped
1 large bunch turnip greens, washed, large stems removed, chiffonade
Salt and pepper
2 cups chicken stock
1 (12-ounce) bottle NOLA Brewing Irish Channel Stout or Guinness
½ tablespoon minced garlic
½ cup Worcestershire sauce
2 tablespoons butter
1 tablespoon brown sugar
1 (2-inch-thick) slice ham (about 6 ounces), cubed
1 teaspoon Tabasco or Crystal hot sauce
1½ cups smoked Gouda cheese, skin removed, cut in ¼-inch cubes or shredded

Cook the bacon over low heat to render as much fat as possible and reserve for another use.

In a large skillet, add the bacon fat and then sauté the onion until brown. Add the chiffonade of greens and cook for 3–4 minutes. Adjust seasoning with salt and pepper. Add the stock, beer, garlic, and Worcestershire, and cook until the greens are tender, but not too mushy. This should take about 15 minutes. (Do not allow them to turn grey in color.)

In a heavy pan, combine the butter and brown sugar. As the mixture starts to bubble, add the ham and toss, sautéing on all sides until nicely cooked. Add the ham to the cooked greens and let simmer for 1 minute. Add the hot sauce and adjust with salt and pepper to taste. Top each serving with 3–4 Gouda cubes.

Maw Maw Lola's Fig Preserves

serves 6 to 8

Water to cover the figs
2–3 cups sugar (depending on
sweetness of the figs)
1 lemon, juiced
1 teaspoon ground cinnamon
2 teaspoons vanilla extract
3–6 cups ripe figs

Bring the water, sugar, lemon, cinnamon, and vanilla to a boil in a large pot over medium-high. Add the figs and reduce the heat to simmer. Allow to simmer for 1–2 hours or until the liquid is reduced by half. Place in sterilized mason jars and follow standard canning procedures.

CHEF to cook

My grandmother Lola had a fig tree on Orchid Street where she lived for 65 years. Every year during my youth, she and I would harvest the figs. Every season the entire family enjoyed her fig preserves—it was truly a gift. I can cook this recipe in my sleep.

Vanilla Iles Flottante with Piña Colada Custard and Pineapple-Caramel Sauce

serves 6 to 8

CUSTARD
4 cups whole milk
²/₃ cup sugar
1 vanilla bean, split with pod scraped into the milk
1 cinnamon stick
1 star anise pod
1 (12-ounce) can coconut milk
12 eggs, separated
2 cups heavy cream
1 teaspoon vanilla extract
1 cup spiced rum

ILES
Generous pinch of salt
1¼ teaspoons sugar
2 teaspoons vanilla extract

Custard In a large saucepan, bring the whole milk to a boil and then add the sugar, vanilla, cinnamon, star anise, and coconut milk. Boil for 1 minute more and then remove from heat, being careful that it does not boil over; cover slightly.

Separate the 12 eggs; reserve the egg whites for the Iles. Place the egg yolks in a stainless steel bowl and whip for 1 minute by hand. Add ⅛ cup of the warm milk mixture into the yolks and stir vigorously. When the yolks have started to temper, incorporate the remaining milk mixture.

Whip the cream, then add cream and vanilla extract to the mixture. Let cool completely and then add the rum.

Iles Beat 11 whites until very stiff. Add the salt, sugar, and vanilla. Pour into a greased deep cake pan and rest in a bain-marie or water bath. Bake at 300 degrees F for 30–50 minutes until lightly browned. Let cool and then carefully remove from the cake pan onto a large plate and refrigerate.

PINEAPPLE-CARAMEL SAUCE
1 (6-ounce) can pineapple juice
1¼ cups sugar
1½ cups heavy cream
1 teaspoon vanilla extract

Pineapple-Caramel Sauce In a heavy 1-quart saucepan, reduce the pineapple juice to 1 tablespoon. Using a fork, combine the sugar with the reduced pineapple juice. This will resemble wet sand. Heat over medium-high heat and do not stir. Cook for 3–6 minutes until the mixture turns a caramel color. (Be very cautious with this mixture as it can burn easily.) Reduce heat to low. Carefully add the cream and mix continuously and vigorously for 1–3 minutes. Add the vanilla and cool before serving.

Assembly Pour the Custard into small bowls and top each with a slice of the molded Iles. Generously drizzle the Pineapple-Caramel Sauce over the top.

Fig and Ice Cream Sandwich with Cream Cheese "Breads" and Candied Peanuts

serves 12

FIG AND ICE CREAM SANDWICH"

⅔ cup Crisco shortening
(preferably butter flavor)
⅔ cup light brown sugar
2 cups all-purpose flour
4 large eggs
2 pounds cream cheese,
room temperature
1 cup sugar
1 teaspoon vanilla extract
1½ teaspoons fresh lemon juice
1¼ tablespoons Madeira Tawny
Sherry
1 gallon vanilla ice cream or any
flavor desired
2 cups fig preserves

Fig and Ice Cream Sandwich Preheat oven to 350 degrees F. Cream shortening and sugar together, then cut in flour. Cut the shortening mixture with pastry cutters; mixture should look like crumbs or wet sand. Spread evenly in a 9½ x 11-inch greased baking pan, and prebake for 15 minutes or until set.

Beat the eggs together in a mixing bowl for about 2 minutes or until a nice lemon color is achieved. Add the cream cheese, sugar, vanilla, lemon juice, and sherry. Beat for another 1–2 minutes or until smooth; set aside.

Spread the filling evenly over the prebaked crust and bake for 15–20 or minutes, until set. Remove the pan and let cool slightly.

Cut into ice cream sandwich rounds, squares or rectangles. Cut the ice cream of your choice, preferably vanilla, into 2 x 2-inch squares and place onto parchment paper; refreeze immediately.

In a separate pot, bring fig preserves to a simmer; let cool and set aside.

CANDIED PEANUTS
2 cups dry roasted, lightly salted
peanuts, coarsely chopped
2 tablespoons unsalted butter
3 tablespoons sugar in the raw
2 teaspoons vanilla extract

WHIPPED CREAM
2 cups heavy cream, chilled well
2 teaspoons sugar
1 teaspoon vanilla extract

Candied Peanuts Briefly sauté the peanuts in the butter for 1 minute over medium-high heat and then add the sugar and vanilla. Cook for 1–2 minutes, tossing the peanuts constantly. When sugar has started to melt, remove the nuts to a parchment-lined pan and let cool completely.

Whipped Cream Combine all ingredients for whipped cream and beat on high for 1–2 minutes, or until soft peaks form.

Assembly Place one piece of the cookie "bread," crust side down, and then place an ice cream square on top. Drizzle with warm fig preserves. Top with another cookie, crust side up. Top with whipped cream and garnish with candied peanuts. Serve immediately.

Left: *A Streetcar Named Desire* (1951)
Directed by Elia Kazan
Shown: Marlon Brando (as
Stanley Kowalski)

Right: Tennessee Williams
on a hotel veranda in
Puerto Vallarta, 1963

FOOD AND RITUALS

The rituals of dining and drinking function to reveal aspects of society and regionalism throughout a number of the plays. In *A Streetcar Named Desire*, Stella has made a birthday cake for Blanche, who is in her early thirties but professes to be younger, and Mitch is scheduled to "come for cake and ice cream." Blanche, a stickler for her own private rituals, insists that "A hot bath and a long cold drink always give one a brand new outlook on life!" The ritual of meal time with the family, once a staple in most regions, sadly out of fashion in our time, is central to *The Glass Menagerie,* in which Amanda Wingfield insists that everyone must be assembled at the table before grace can be said. Ever the stickler for religious niceties, Amanda, when she discovers that the gentleman caller who will be coming to dinner has an Irish name, concludes, "That, of course means fish—tomorrow is Friday! I'll have that salmon loaf—with Durkees dressing!" (Those of us of a certain age know that when Amanda talks of salmon, she means the canned variety.)

Gayden Metcalf and Charlotte Hays have brilliantly evoked for us in *Being Dead Is No Excuse*, the Southern tradition of bringing food to the home of a bereaved family, and a variation on that ritual occurs in *Battle of Angels* and its later revised version, *Orpheus Descending*. When Myra (in *Battle of Angels*) is bringing her husband Jabe home from the hospital following unsuccessful cancer surgery, relatives and townspeople gather with food (in *Orpheus Descending* her name is Lady): Beulah Binnings brings floating island and a pie ("the meringue turned out real good") and Vee Talbot brings sherbet–"something light and digestible"–which unfortunately melted as she brought it through the Delta heat. There are also olive nut sandwiches, which Sister, a cousin of Jabe's, takes with her when she leaves, to serve at the "Bishop's tea," to which "the Bishop Adjutant is coming"—yet another Southern Episcopal ritual. In *A Streetcar Named Desire*, Blanche makes custard, a tried and true Southern comfort food, for Mitch's ailing mother. And there are rituals involving liquor: for example, in *Battle of Angels*, Cassandra says that she pours whiskey on her great-aunt's grave, because she had "loved to drink" so much that she finally stayed in bed all the time doing nothing else. I'm sure that Noel Polk can tell us about the same ceremony performed at William Faulkner's grave in Oxford by students and their professor.

Birthdays and other holidays are symbolically significant in many of the dramas. The most bizarre birthday extravaganza in all the plays occurs in *Cat on a Hot Tin Roof*, in which yet another man has come home following cancer surgery, this time Big Daddy, surely the greatest male character Tennessee ever created, and the family, including his doting wife, two sons—Brick, a former college football jock, and Gooper, a corporate attorney—and their ambitious wives, Maggie and Mae, aka Sister Woman, and a passel of "no-neck monsters" assemble for what many of them, but not Big Daddy, know will be his last birthday celebration. When Maggie the Cat complains about the behavior of the no-neck monsters, Mae insists that the children, bad mannered though they may be, must be at the table because it's Big Daddy's birthday, where a cake is served with "buckets of champagne."

Sometimes the ritual of eating and drinking evokes humor in the plays, as in *Something Unspoken*, when the authoritarian Cornelia asks Esmeralda Hawkins by phone what is being served at the Confederate Daughters meeting: "Chicken a la king! Wouldn't you know? That is so characteristic of poor Amelia! With bits of pimiento and tiny mushrooms in it?. . . And afterwards I suppose there was lemon sherbet with lady fingers! What, lime sherbet! And no lady fingers? What a departure! What a shocking *apostasy*! I'm quite stunned!" Similarly, in *Out Cry*, Clare complains to her brother about "violet-haired Drama Club Ladies" eating "*Vol-au-vent* and *Peche Melba*." And in *Camino Real*, Kilroy, set on winning the Gypsy's daughter Esmeralda, tells her, ". . . that's the way we do things in the States. A little vino, some records on the victrola, some quiet conversation—and then if both parties are in a mood for romance . . . Romance—."

Despite the tragic quality of most of his plays, Tennessee Williams, like Shakespeare before him, knew how to alleviate the gloom with humor, one element that serves to lift his best work above others. Sometimes that humor is related to, even achieved through, a connection to food and drink. In *Cat on a Hot Tin Roof*, for example, after Big Mama, having listened to complaints about her son Brick's drinking, asserts that "Other people *drink* and *have* drunk an' will *drink* as long at they

Upper: *Orpheus Descending* (1957 Broadway)
Play by Tennessee Williams
Directed by Harold Clurman
Shown: Playbill

Lower: *Camino Real* (1960 Off-Broadway revival)
Play by Tennessee Williams
Directed by Jose Quintero
Shown: Playgram

make that stuff and put it in bottles" and when Maggie adds, "I never trusted a man that didn't drink," the clueless Sister Woman proudly asserts of her husband, "Gooper never drinks." Maggie does not even have to respond, for Sister Woman is clearly "hoist on her own petard." There are many such brief flashes of comic effect, as when the Witch of Capri in *The Milk Train Doesn't Stop Here Anymore* replies to Flora Goforth's offer of "a gull's egg" by saying, "I can't stand gulls" and Flora responds, "Well, eating their eggs cuts down on their population." To convince Dr. John Buchanan to come to her "literary" gathering, Alma tells him, "We *will* have punch, fruit punch, with claret in it. Do you like claret?" The sarcasm of John's response—"I just dote on claret"—seems to be lost on Alma. In *A Lovely Sunday for Creve Coeur*, the perceptive but unpolished Bodey suggests that Ralph got Dorothea drunk on a flask of liquor, to which Dorothea replies, "Drunk on a single Pink Lady?— The mildest sort of cocktail! Made with sloe gin and grenadine."

Bodey: The gin was slow, maybe, but that man is a fast one.

Gutman, the hotel proprietor in *Camino Real*, suggests to Casanova a "very cold and dry" wine called "Quando!–meaning when! Such as 'when are remittances to be received?' 'When are accounts to be settled?'" In *Night of the Iguana*, Shannon claims that the drunken cook at the rundown Costa Verde hotel is from Shanghai and "handled the kitchen at an exclusive club there . . . he's a bug, a fanatic about—what!—continental cuisine—can even make Beef Stroganoff and thermidor dishes." Similarly, the Gypsy in *Camino Real*, quotes an old Chinese proverb: "When your goose is cooked you might as well have it cooked with plenty of gravy."

In addition to humor, Tennessee's plays are rich in poetry, so much so that a television documentary on his life referred to him as "An American Orpheus." Food and poetry often commingle in the dramas, as a

IN *SMALL CRAFT WARNINGS*, LEONA
PREPARES A "MEMORIAL
DINNER" FOR BILL: "LAMB STEW WITH FRESH GREEN
VEGETABLES FROM THE FARMER'S
MARKET SEASONED WITH BAY LEAVES, ROSEMARY AND THYME."

TOWER'S CORK & WOOD PENHOLDER PAT

few examples indicate. In *I Rise in Flame Cried the Phoenix*, when D. H. Lawrence finds a jar of marmalade an admirer has left on his steps, he observes that "This is the month of August put in a bottle." A recurrent metaphor is one Tennessee must have learned in Sicily: *The Rose Tattoo*, dedicated to his Sicilian lover Frank Merlo, contains an exchange between two main characters:

Seraphina: Your glass is weeping.
Mangiacavallo: Your glass is weeping too.

The same symbol is repeated in the late play, *Vieux Carre*, when Jane, the New Yorker, says, "Oh, my glass is weeping—an Italian expression."

So imbued was Thomas Lanier Williams, the "preacher's boy," in the rites of the church, that religious ritual figures significantly in the plays. In *Out Cry*, Celeste tells her brother, "Bread is something that has to be broken in kindness, in friendship or understanding, as it was broken among the Apostles at Our Lord's Last Supper." In *The Milk Train Doesn't Stop Here Anymore*, Christopher Flanders has been starving for days when he arrives at Flora Goforth's villa on Capri, where he continues to be denied food. When he is finally given a bottle of milk, "he sips the milk as if it were sacrificial wine," a passage that helps to explain the title of the play. In *Small Craft Warnings*, Leona prepares a "memorial dinner" for Bill: "Lamb stew with fresh green vegetables from the farmer's market, seasoned with bay leaves, and rosemary and thyme." A perverse and horrifying reversal of a religious ritual appears in *Vieux Carre*, when Tye relates to Jane the fact that the Bourbon Street stripper called "the Champagne Girl" has been eaten by the fierce Italian dogs owned by the Mafia boss: "Those lupos ate that kid like she was their last supper. . . ." And in *Suddenly Last Summer*, Catherine relates the gory story of how the starving children in Cabeza de Lobo, who had earlier chanted *"Pan, pan, pan!"* to indicate their hunger, killed her cousin Sebastian and *"devoured* parts of him," a variation on the death of Saint Sebastian and an oblique illusion to the Last Supper. In a reference to a miracle performed by Christ, a drunken Tom, having stumbled home late at night, tells his sister Laura in *The Glass Menagerie* that he saw a movie followed by a stage show in which "Malvolio the Magician" turned water "to wine and then it turned to beer and then it turned to whiskey." He knows it was whiskey because he volunteered from the audience to test it during both shows: "It was Kentucky Straight Bourbon."

Drink plays a significant ritualistic part of several productions, for example, in *Suddenly Last Summer*, when Catherine observes, "There goes the Waring Mixer. Aunt Violet's about to have her five o'clock frozen daiquiri, you could set a watch by it." In Tennessee's most religious play, *Night of the Iguana*, Shannon, the defrocked Episcopal priest, chides the proprietress of the Costa Verde Hotel, for failing to respect the proper order of meal courses: "People don't drink cocktails between the fish and the entree, Maxine honey," he says, to which Maxine replies that she is making a Manhattan for the elderly poet Nonno: "Old folks need a toddy to pick 'em up." In a variation on the eastern tea ritual, Hannah Jelkes prepares a cup of poppyseed tea with sugared ginger to calm the distraught Shannon; "Blue Devils," she says, "respect all the truth that panicky people use to outlast and outwit their panic. . . Poppy seed tea or rum cocos or just a few deep

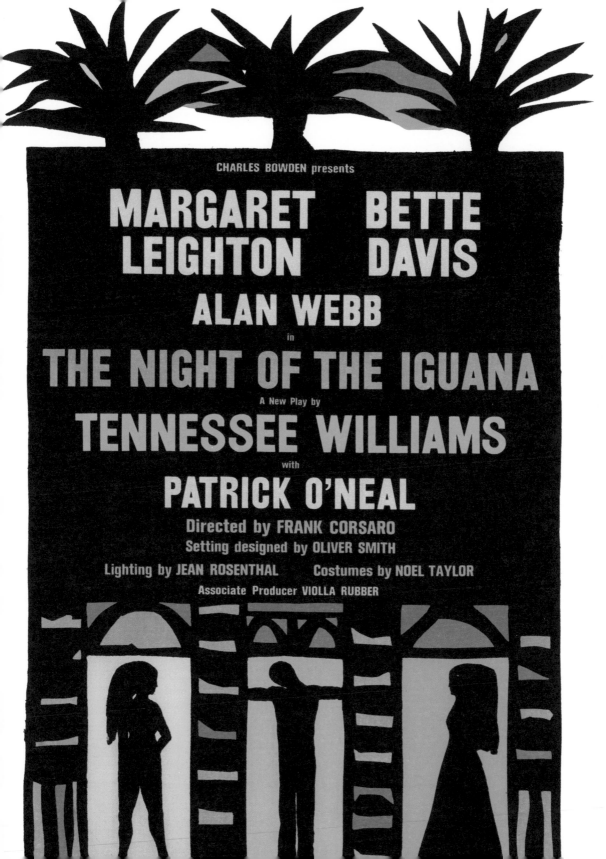

The Milk Train Doesn't Stop Here Anymore (Stage revival, Brooks Atkinson Theatre, NY, Jan. 1-4, 1964) Play by Tennessee Williams Directed by Tony Richardson Shown on Playbill cover: Tallulah Bankhead

breaths." In the same play, set in 1940, the German tourists at the Costa Verde take a case of Carta Blanca beer to the beach to celebrate the fire-bombing of London, and in *The Milk Train Doesn't Stop Here Anymore*, the Witch of Capri downs a pitcher of martinis, insisting that "Liquor improves my concentration."

Given all this food and drink, it is not surprising that occasionally, Tennessee Williams would submit himself to a dietary regimen, cutting back for health's sake; his letters are filled with announcements that he is now drinking "only one or two drinks a day and eating very frugally." These periods were brief and rather far between. In his college years, he wrote to his mother from Iowa that he was looking for some other place to eat since "The diet at Scott's is too starchy: potatoes three times a day, seven days a week." He professes on one occasion to having borrowed money from his fellow ATO's "to continue eating which is an annoyingly persistent habit, especially in these northern climates." In the plays, various characters undergo similar restrictions—or plan to; for example, in *Kingdom of Earth*, Myrtle tells her brother-in-law, "Now what I want most in the world is to return to show business! . . . I'm going to cut out all fats and sweets and fried foods and get back my shape." A pattern for the healthy life is put forth by Violet Venable in *Suddenly Last Summer* in describing the asceticism of her son Sebastian:: "It takes character to refuse to grow old, Doctor—successfully to refuse to. It calls for discipline, abstention. One cocktail before dinner, not two, four, six—a single lean chop and lime juice on a salad in restaurants famed for rich dishes."

The plays of Tennessee Williams are always imbued with sex, and like many another author, he often combines that motif with food and drink. In *Twenty-Seven Wagons Full of Cotton*, Jake inquires of his wife Baby Doll, "What would I do if you was a big piece of cake? What would I do if you was angel food cake? Big white piece with lots of nice thick icin'."

The unnamed male protagonist of *Talk to Me Like the Rain and Let Me Listen* describes a party at which he was drunk and "When I woke up I was naked in a bathtub full of melting ice-cubes." The other character, a woman, counters his story by saying that she has been living on water and instant coffee. Here drink provides the sharp contrast between the life of excess and the life of abstention. The sexual tension is palpable in *The Rose Tattoo* between Seraphina Delle Rosa and Alvaro, who arrives at her home on the Mississippi Gulf Coast after his truck has been driven off the highway; like her dead husband, he drives a banana delivery truck—in this play, no one eats anything except bananas and chocolate, no pasta, oddly enough, and the only drink is wine. The last name of Alvaro, a man of great appetites, is Mangiacavallo, which translates "Eat a Horse," a sexual allusion personal to Tennessee Williams.

Suddenly, Last Summer (1959) Directed by Joseph L. Mankiewicz Shown on poster, from left: Elizabeth Taylor, Montgomery Clift, Katherine Hepburn

Not surprisingly, the drama with the most sexual elements is *A Streetcar Named Desire*, for it was in the city of New Orleans and particularly the French Quarter that the playwright encountered the promiscuity and license he previously had not known existed. Of Stanley, the stage directions say that *"Animal joy in his being is implicit in all his movements and manhood."* In the opening scene of *Streetcar*, Stanley tosses a blood-stained package wrapped in butcher's paper to his wife, yelling, "Catch."

Stella: What?

Stanley: Meat.

The sexual implications of this exchange between the couple might pass unnoticed but for the comments of a neighbor woman, who asks Eunice, the landlady, "What was that package he th'ew at 'er?" to which Eunice replies, "You hush, now!" "Catch *what!*" the unnamed neighbor asks, laughing raucously. Later, Blanche describes her brother-in-law in terms that unconsciously refer back to this first scene: "Stanley Kowalski—survivor of the stone age! Bearing the raw meat home from the kill in the jungle!"

One seemingly innocent scene that actually seethes with sexual tension occurs between Blanche DuBois and the unnamed young man come to collect for the delivery of the newspaper:

Blanche: Didn't you get wet in the rain?

Young Man: No ma'am I stepped inside.

Blanche: In a drug store? And had a soda?

Young Man: Uh-hun.

Blanche: Chocolate?

Young Man: No ma'am. Cherry.

Blanche: Cherry.

Young Man: A cherry soda.

Blanche: You make my mouth water.

The encounter ends when, after a kiss, Blanche sends him on his way, saying "It would be nice to keep you, but I've got to be good—and keep my hands off children."

A STREETCAR NAMED DESIRE

Chop Suey Soup

1 chicken breast, sliced in thin strips
Salt and pepper
1 cup cornstarch
1/4 cup peanut oil for frying
2 carrots, peeled and diagonally sliced
2 ribs celery, diagonally sliced
1 large onion, thinly sliced
1 red pepper, julienned
2 quarts chicken stock (preferably homemade)
1 1/2 cups lite soy sauce
1 teaspoon Chinese 5-spice powder
1 teaspoon ground ginger
6 cloves garlic, thinly sliced
2 (12-ounce) cans Chinese vegetable blend, drained
1 package ramen noodles, cooked
1/2 cup hoisin sauce
1/2 bunch green onions, diagonally sliced

Season chicken with salt and pepper; dust lightly with cornstarch and shake off excess. Heat oil in a soup pot and then sauté the chicken for 1 minute and remove.

Add the vegetables, except for the Chinese canned mix and the green onions. Sauté the vegetables until the onion is translucent. Add the stock, soy sauce, 5-spice powder, ginger, and garlic. Cook over low heat for 30 minutes.

Return the chicken to the pot and cook for 1 minute, or until the thin strips of chicken are cooked. Add the canned vegetables. Deep fry cooked noodles in the peanut oil, drain, and drizzle with hoisin and salt.

Place the soup in bowls and top with fried noodles and the green onion tops.

"Red Hots" Tamales

serves 6 to 8

MASA (DOUGH)
1 pound (approximately 4 cups)
masa harina (tortilla flour)
8½ cups water
1½ teaspoons kosher salt
4 tablespoons shortening

FILLING
1 pound ground pork
1 pound ground beef
1 medium onion, finely chopped
1 teaspoon minced garlic
2 pounds ripe tomatoes, chopped
1 teaspoon unsweetened cocoa powder
1½ teaspoons dry red pepper flakes
1 small poblano pepper, finely chopped
½ cup minced red bell pepper
Salt and pepper
Corn husks for wrapping tamales

Masa (dough) Combine all the ingredients for the dough in a large pot. Cook over low heat for approximately 35–40 minutes, stirring constantly to prevent sticking.

Filling In a large skillet, brown beef and pork slightly then add the onion, garlic, tomatoes, cocoa powder, dry red pepper flakes, poblano pepper, and red pepper and cook for about 15 minutes. Adjust seasoning with salt and pepper.

Assembly Using a corn husk, place masa in the center. Spread it out over the husk, then add 4–5 table-spoons filling down the center of the masa. Wrap to cover filling. Tie with a string or simply wrap in aluminum foil sheets. Repeat until masa and filling are all used up. Place tamales in a steamer and steam for 1½ hours. Serve.

CHEF to cook

The tamales Tennessee references in *A Streetcar Named Desire* were cooked and wrapped in corn husks. Husks are available at Latin grocery stores. Banana leaves may be substituted.

Grilled Watermelon, Pickled Carrots, Grapes, and Romaine Salad with Watermelon Cracklin's

serves 6

PICKLING INGREDIENTS
1 quart seasoned rice wine vinegar
2 cinnamon sticks
1 tablespoon 7-spice powder*
2 tablespoons peppercorn mélange (optional)
2 whole cloves
3 star anise flowers
12 cloves garlic, peeled and ends trimmed
2 cups sugar
1 lemon, zested

WATERMELON CRACKLIN'S
3 large carrots, peeled
1 medium watermelon
1 cup lite soy sauce
1 tablespoon smoked sea salt
1 egg
½ cup milk
6 cups semolina
Peanut oil for frying

This can be found at Middle Eastern markets.

Pickling Ingredients Combine all of the pickling ingredients in a saucepan. Bring to a boil and then simmer over low heat for 10 minutes.

Watermelon Cracklin's Slice the carrots into shoestring size with a mandolin. Peel the melon and cut the flesh into 2 x 3-inch rectangles; reserve for grilling and also reserve rinds. Place the carrots in a heatproof bowl with a lid and ladle liquid of the pickling mixture into the bowl to cover the carrots. Place all of the garlic, peppers, and spices into the container with the carrots as well.

Add an equal part water to the pot with the remaining pickling liquid. Add soy sauce and salt. Add the melon rinds and cook over low heat for 1–2 hours, or until rinds are soft and tender, but not mushy. Drain and dry the rinds.

Mix the egg with the milk in a mixing bowl. Toss the dry rinds into the egg mixture and then dredge in the semolina. Fry in peanut oil at 375 degrees F until golden brown. Drain on a kitchen towel.

continued on page 102

SALAD
Extra virgin olive oil
Salt and pepper
Romaine lettuce
1 pound grapes

Salad Coat the watermelon chunks with olive oil, and salt and pepper and grill both sides briefly. Chiffonade the Romaine leaves; season with salt and pepper and olive oil. Wash and slice the grapes.

Assembly Place the lettuce on the bottom of the plate and then add the carrots. Drizzle a little of the pickling juice. Place the watermelon on top. Sprinkle the salad with the grapes and garlic cloves, and top with the watermelon rind cracklin's.

CHEF to cook

It is best to do the pickling
a couple of days ahead.
The longer the items can
marinate, the better.

Oyster Fritters with Asparagus Tips and Minted Green Peas with Cream

serves 6 to 10

FRITTERS
4 tablespoons chopped onion
4 tablespoons extra virgin olive oil
1/2 pound bacon, cooked
18 fresh Louisiana oysters
3 teaspoons chopped garlic
1 tablespoon Worcestershire sauce
Salt and pepper
Peanut oil for frying

BATTER
1 cup all-purpose flour
1 tablespoon baking powder
2 eggs
1 teaspoon salt
1/4 teaspoon cayenne pepper
Liquid from fritters mixture plus
enough milk to equal 2/3 cup

PEAS AND ASPARAGUS
18 asparagus spears
4 cups fresh English Peas (frozen
may be substituted)
6 tablespoons unsalted butter
3 cups heavy cream
1 tablespoon chopped mint
Salt and pepper

Fritters Sauté the onion in the olive oil with the bacon until onion is tender. Add the oysters, Worcestershire, and garlic; sauté for 1 minute and remove.

Batter Mix all of the batter ingredients together in a mixing bowl. Use some of the juice from the oyster batter first and then finish with the milk.

Peas and Asparagus Blanch the asparagus spears in salted water until almost tender. Cook the peas in butter and cream until tender. Add the mint and adjust seasoning with salt and pepper. Add the asparagus and keep warm.

Finish and Assembly Over moderate heat, heat approximately enough peanut oil to cover one-fourth of a cast-iron skillet. Combine the fritter mixture with the batter. Form dough into fritters, approximately 1 tablespoon per fritter (3 oysters each). Cook the first side of the fritter in the hot oil until almost done in the center. Carefully flip the fritter to finish the other side. You can fry more than one fritter at a time, but don't crowd the pan. Serve on plate with the peas and asparagus cream sauce.

 CHEF to cook

This is Blanche's dinner.

That Spaghetti Dish "Dirty Rice" Pasta

serves 6 to 8

1 pound lean ground beef
Salt and pepper
4 whole duck livers, diced
1 jumbo onion, finely chopped
1 red bell pepper, finely chopped
1 large green bell pepper, finely chopped
2 ribs celery, finely chopped
6 green onions, chopped with whites separated from the green
1 (8-ounce) can beef stock
4 cloves garlic, minced
3 tablespoons Worcestershire sauce
1 cup veal demi-glace
1 tablespoon tamarind paste (optional)
1–1½ pounds fettuccine

Brown the beef for 2–3 minutes and season lightly with salt and pepper. Remove beef from the pan and add the duck livers; sauté for 1 minute and remove to plate with the beef.

Add and sauté the vegetables except for the green onions. Deglaze with beef stock. Add garlic, Worcestershire, demi-glace, and white tops of the green onions. Add tamarind paste if using. Simmer until vegetables are al dente. Add beef and livers to finish cooking, approximately 2 minutes.

Cook fettuccine in a large pot with salted water, then drain and place in large heatproof bowl. Add meat sauce and toss. Garnish with green parts of green onions and serve.

Mississippi Boiled Custard or Crème Anglaise

serves 10 to 12

3 cups whole milk
1 cup sugar
2 tablespoons all-purpose flour
1/8 teaspoon salt
4 eggs
1 cup heavy cream
1 tablespoon vanilla
3–4 tablespoons good bourbon or brandy

Scald the milk in a pot and then allow to cool a bit.

Blend the dry ingredients in a mixing bowl; beat eggs and then whisk into the dry ingredients. Add the scalded milk and heavy cream. (In a pinch, evaporated milk may be substituted.)

Cook in a double boiler over medium heat, stirring constantly, until the mixture coats the back of a spoon. Remember that it will thicken as it cools.

To be sure that the custard is smooth, beat it with an electric mixture. Allow to cool more and then mix in the vanilla and the Bourbon or brandy. When the mixture is cooled sufficiently, refrigerate, covered.

The French called it "Crème Anglaise." The French's even deigning to notice an English food item without a sneer, much less giving it a title, is amazing. The Anglo-Saxons and Celtic immigrants who settled the American South brought the dish with them as a staple dessert, and so it has remained, for the most part, through the more than three centuries since.

When I was growing up, it was always served with the winter holiday meals—Thanksgiving and Christmas—but it was also made whenever it was needed, throughout the year, as a "comfort food," a salve to the soul of an ill child or adult, and thus it brought on a kind of mystical aura that remains to this day.

When I was grown and my mother was lost to me, taking with her in her sadly hasty exit from this earth many of the recipes for dishes that I had loved and always assumed would be with me throughout my life, I finally turned to the task of learning how to make that Crème Anglaise, or, "Boiled Custard." It proved not to be difficult to make but only to require close attention and, I suppose, a love inspired by abiding memories.

—Recipe courtesy of Kenneth Holditch

Grilled Peach, Cherry, and Pecan Bread Pudding with Goat Cheese Caramel and Southern Comfort

serves 12

BREAD PUDDING
1 cup sun-dried cherries
1½ cups Southern Comfort liqueur
8 ripe peaches
10 tablespoons unsalted butter, divided
2 cups sugar, divided
1 tablespoon ground cinnamon
¼ tablespoon nutmeg
1½ cups coarsely chopped pecans
1–2 loaves French bread, torn in pieces
4 cups half-and-half
2 tablespoons vanilla extract
4 eggs, beaten
1 cup shredded coconut

CARAMEL
1 pound sugar
½ cup Southern Comfort liqueur
3 tablespoons water
½ lemon, juiced
2 cups heavy cream
3–4 ounces goat cheese

Bread Pudding Soak the cherries in the liquor for 1 hour. Peel peaches, quarter, and lightly grill on all sides. Dice 4 of the peaches for the pudding and slice 4 for the sauce. Set aside peaches for sauce.

Melt butter, add ½ cup sugar, cinnamon, nutmeg, and pecans. Toss together and sauté mixture over medium heat for 2 minutes. Remove the nuts.

Add cherries with liqueur, peaches, and butter in a pan and sauté for 2 minutes; let cool slightly.

Combine the bread, half-and-half, remaining sugar, vanilla, and eggs in a large bowl and let soak for 30 minutes, until the liquid is absorbed. Mush together until achieving a smooth consistency. Fold in coconut and cooked fruit mixture with juices. Place in a greased high-sided 9-inch loaf pan and compress. Bake for 45 minutes to 1 hour at 350 degrees F, until a toothpick inserted in the center comes out clean. Let cool before removing from the pan and slicing.

Caramel Combine the sugar, liquor, water, and lemon juice in a heavy saucepan. The mixture should resemble coarse sand. Place pan over medium heat and let ingredients melt. Do not stir, but lightly shake to mix. In 2–5 minutes, mixture should be a light caramel color. Remove from heat and add the cream. Whip until smooth and cream is incorporated. Add the goat cheese, stir in until smooth, and cool.

SAUCE

8 tablespoons unsalted butter
1 cup light brown sugar, tightly packed
1 vanilla bean, scraped
1 (6-ounce) can peach nectar
²/₃ cup Southern Comfort liqueur

Sauce Combine the butter, brown sugar, vanilla, peach nectar, and liqueur in a saucepan. Cook until thickened slightly, about 5 minutes over high heat. Add the sliced peaches and warm through, then add remaining liqueur and carefully flame.

Assembly Place a slice of the bread pudding on a plate, top with the flamed peach sauce, and drizzle with caramel. Optionally, place a scoop of vanilla ice cream on top of pudding before drizzling the sauce.

CAMINO REAL

Smoked Corn and Grilled Pepper Bisque with Tequila, Lemon, and Salt-Flavored Tortilla Chips

serves 6

BISQUE

4 ears fresh corn
1 large red bell pepper
1 large poblano pepper
1/2 pound chorizo
3 quarts chicken stock
2 large onions, diced
1 large green bell pepper, diced
3 ribs celery, diced
2 tablespoons olive oil
3 tablespoons minced garlic
1 tablespoon cilantro
2 tablespoons Worcestershire sauce
1 teaspoon cumin
1/4 teaspoon ground cinnamon
1/2 teaspoon dark chili powder
1 large loaf stale French bread
2 cups heavy cream

Bisque Roast the corn in their husks for 10 minutes, remove, and when cool enough to handle, cut the kernels from the corn. Reserve the cobs for smoking.

Grill the red bell pepper and poblano for about 2 minutes per side. Remove from the grill, deseed, dice, and set aside.

Roast the chorizo in an oven at 450 degrees F for 6 minutes. Remove, let drain on paper towels, and then slice into 1/2-inch rounds and set aside.

Smoke the reserved cobs either on a stovetop or outdoors for 40 minutes until a deep caramel color. In a large pot, add the cobs to the chicken stock and cook for 5–7 minutes over medium heat.

Sauté the vegetables in the olive oil over low heat until the onions have softened, about 6 minutes. Add the sautéed vegetables to the stock along with two-thirds of the corn kernels, garlic, cilantro, Worcestershire, cumin, cinnamon, chili powder, and the loaf of bread with the crust removed and torn in pieces. Cook over

continued on page 112

TORTILLA CHIPS

6 corn tortillas, sliced into
½-inch strips
Peanut oil for frying
1 lemon, juiced
1 tablespoon tequila
1 teaspoon kosher salt

low heat for 40 minutes, or until all the vegetables are tender. Remove and discard cobs.

In several batches, puree the mixture and strain through fine mesh. Return to the pot. After fully pureed, add the remaining corn and diced peppers to the soup. Follow with the cream and chorizo. Adjust seasoning with salt and pepper. Let simmer for another 5 minutes, stirring occasionally.

Tortilla Chips Fry tortilla strips in hot oil until crispy. Remove and drain on paper towels. Season with lemon juice, tequila, and salt.

To Serve Ladle bisque into soup bowls, garnish with the tortilla strips, and serve.

TEQUILA

COMES FROM THE BLUE AGAVE GROWN IN THE

MEXICAN STATES OF

JALISCO, OR IN PARTS OF MICHOACÁN OR TAMAULIPAS, NAYARIT, AND GUANAJUATO.

AUTHENTIC TEQUILA must have a minimum of 51 percent certified blue agave in it. Tequila lends a very unique profile to foods packing a flavorful punch, pairing beautifully with citrus. It enhances spices like cilantro, oregano, and garlic yielding that unexpected layer of piquancy.

Roast Duck Breast Biscuit with Huevos Fritos

serves 6

2 large red onions, sliced
Salt and pepper
1 cup honey
2 cups balsamic vinegar
1 cinnamon stick
5 duck breasts, cold smoked
2 medium onions, sliced
1 cup semolina
4 tablespoons peanut oil
6 eggs
3 cups fresh spinach
1 teaspoon nutmeg
6 biscuits, preferably homemade

In a large, heavy-bottomed skillet, add two-thirds of the red onions and sauté in peanut oil over low heat. Add a good pinch of salt and the onions will start to give up their juice. Raise the heat to medium and lightly brown. Add honey, vinegar, and the cinnamon stick. Cook over low heat for 12–15 minutes until onions are fully cooked. Adjust seasoning with salt and pepper. Keep warm.

Roast the cold-smoked duck breasts at 475 degrees F for 6 minutes. Flesh should be firm; remove and rest. Reserve fat. Toss remaining onions with the semolina and fry in the peanut oil until crispy. Season with salt and pepper and remove from pan.

Fry eggs in the oil and season with salt and pepper. Sauté the spinach in the reserved duck fat with nutmeg and salt and pepper.

Split and place warm biscuits on plate, open-face style. Place generous amount of the battered onions on biscuits and top with sliced duck breasts. Place 1 fried egg on top and sprinkle with the fried red onions. Arrange the sautéed spinach in a circle around the biscuit and serve.

Basic Southern-Style Biscuit

makes 12

1 package dried yeast
1/4 cup very warm water
2 1/2 tablespoons sugar, divided
2 1/4–2 1/2 cups flour
1/2 tablespoon baking soda
1 1/2 tablespoons baking powder
1–2 teaspoons salt
1/2 cup Crisco or butter-flavored shortening
1 cup whole milk

Place yeast in warm water with 1/2 teaspoon of the sugar (this helps feed the yeast and accelerate the bubbles) and stir. Let stand 2–4 minutes in a warm spot in the kitchen.

Blend the dry ingredients and then cut in shortening and mix. Add yeast and milk and incorporate. Knead slightly and form a ball. Place ball into a lightly greased bowl and cover with a damp, clean kitchen towel. Let rise for about 1 hour in the warmest, draft-free area of the kitchen.

Turn out dough onto a lightly floured board (1/4 cup flour). Roll into a 1 1/4–2 inch symmetrically shaped cylinder. Cut dough into rounds and let rise about 3 minutes. Bake in a convection oven at 400 degrees F for 10–12 minutes, or until golden brown. Serve with butter or syrup.

As a variation, add 1/4 cup of grated pepper jack cheese to the dry mixture.

Grilled Pork Paillard Tacos with Red Onion, Paneed Pineapple, Queso Fresco Sour Cream, and "Fritos"

serves 6

GRILLED PORK TACOS AND
PANEED PINEAPPLE
1½ pounds center loin boneless
pork
Salt and pepper
3 tablespoons extra virgin olive oil
1 tablespoon minced garlic
8 pineapple rings, cut in
1-inch cubes
½ teaspoon garlic powder
½ teaspoon chili powder
1 teaspoon cumin
Peanut oil for frying
All-purpose flour
Egg wash
Breadcrumbs
1 lime, juiced
1 large red onion, thinly sliced
1 tablespoon olive oil
6 corn taco shells
Tabasco sauce (optional)
Romaine lettuce, chiffonade
3 tomatoes, chopped
2 tablespoons chopped fresh
cilantro

Grilled Pork Tacos and Paneed Pineapple Slice pork into ½-inch slices. Pound down to ⅛ inch thickness with a meat mallet. Season with salt and pepper, and lightly coat with the olive oil and minced garlic. Marinate for 5 minutes.

Season the pineapple with salt and pepper, garlic powder, chili powder, and cumin. Dredge in flour, then egg wash, and finally the breadcrumbs. Fry in oil at 375 degrees F until golden brown. Remove and keep warm.

Place pork on hot grill for about 1 minute per side; the meat will cook in seconds so be exact. Remove and season with lime juice, then julienne. Sauté sliced onion in olive oil over high heat with salt and pepper until tender, about 4 minutes.

QUESO FRESCO SOUR CREAM
2 cups sour cream
Juice of ½ lemon
½ cup queso fresco

"FRITOS"
6 large potatoes, peeled and
soaked in ice bath
10 quarts cold, salted water
Peanut oil for frying
Salt and pepper

Queso Fresco Sour Cream Mix sour cream with lemon juice and queso fresco to make Queso Fresco Sour Cream.

"Fritos" Slice potatoes into 1½-inch rounds and put in a pot of cold, salted water. Bring to a boil, checking potatoes every few minutes. As soon as skewer-tender, drain and let dry. Potatoes should be very tender, so they are close to breaking but do not break. Deep fry at 375 degrees F until golden. Season with salt and pepper.

To Serve Place julienne of pork into tacos shells and top with fried pineapple and onion. Add a teaspoon of Tabasco to each taco, if using, and top with lettuce, tomato, and Queso Fresco Sour Cream. Serve with "Fritos." Garnish with the fresh chopped cilantro.

Paneed Lamb Tenderloin with Grilled Pineapple, Avocado, and Green Salad with a Smoked Tomato Vinaigrette

serves 6

LAMB TENDERLOIN AND
GRILLED PINEAPPLE
8 rings fresh pineapple, grilled
and diced
6 (4- to 6-ounce) lamb tenderloins
All-purpose flour, seasoned with
salt and pepper
Egg wash
Breadcrumbs
Peanut oil for frying

SALAD
6 cups mesclun blend salad mix
Salt and pepper
1 large ripe avocado
6 roma or beefsteak tomatoes,
sliced into 6 slices per tomato

VINAIGRETTE
8 roma tomatoes, cut in half
lengthwise
1 tablespoon minced garlic
1/2 cup apple cider vinegar or
red wine vinegar
2 limes, juiced
1 1/2 cups pure olive oil
Salt and pepper

Lamb Tenderloin and Grilled Pineapple Grill pineapple slices for about 3 minutes per side, dice, and then set aside. Dredge lamb in flour, then egg wash, and then finish with breadcrumbs. Deep fry in peanut oil heated to 375 degrees F until golden and medium to medium-rare, about 3 minutes.

Salad Arrange greens seasoned with salt and pepper and moisten with the tomato and lime vinaigrette. Arrange avocado and tomato slices and diced pineapple around the plate.

Smoked Tomato Vinaigrette Smoke the halved tomatoes on a stovetop or grill until they are cooked and soft. Remove and puree tomatoes until smooth. Strain to remove seeds. Return pulp to blender and add the garlic, vinegar, and lime juice; blend. While blending, add the olive oil in a slow stream to emulsify. Add salt and pepper to taste.

CHEF to cook

When smoking, use your favorite flavor chips or herb stems, which add great flavor.

Roasted Banana and Yam Sorbet

serves 6

1 pound yams
1 pound bananas
1 cup water
¾ cup sugar
1¼ teaspoons pectin
½ cup sweetened pineapple juice
1 large lemon, juiced
1 vanilla bean, scraped
½ teaspoon vanilla extract

Roast yams for 1 hour in an oven preheated to 400 degrees F. Add unpeeled bananas to the yams and roast for 30 minutes, or until yams are tender and bananas are soft. Remove from heat and let cool. When cool enough to handle, peel yams and bananas, then mash and whip in a mixing bowl.

Bring the water, sugar, pectin, and juices to a boil. Add scraped vanilla bean to the syrup. Pour hot syrup into whipped yam and banana mixture. Whip by hand for 1–2 minutes, then add vanilla extract. Cool completely to room temperature, and then refrigerate for 1 hour before processing in an ice cream maker.

CHEF to cook

Delicious alone or when served with the Crêpes Suzette, on page 121.

Basic Crêpe

serves 6

2 cups all-purpose flour
2 teaspoons sugar
¼ teaspoon salt
4 eggs, beaten
1 cup half-and-half
1 cup water
¼ cup butter, melted
Peanut oil for cooking

Sift together flour, sugar, and salt. Mix eggs with the half-and-half and water and pour and whisk liquids into flour a little at a time. When all ingredients are combined, add melted butter. Refrigerate for 2–4 hours. Heat crêpe pan or medium saucepan. Brush or spray pan with oil spray and let pan get to almost smoking hot. Pour 4 tablespoons batter into pan, swirl to coat pan so that the batter is spread evenly and very thin. Cook for 1 minute, flip, and cook on the other side for 1 minute. Place on plate and cool. Crêpes can be prepared in advance.

Crêpes Suzette "Café Brulot Style"

serves 6

1½ cups sugar, divided
6 ounces dark chicory coffee
1 cinnamon stick, ground
2 whole cloves, ground
1 vanilla bean, split and scraped
4 tablespoons high-quality or homemade orange marmalade
1 orange, peeled and sliced
6 tablespoons butter, divided
6 ounces Metaxas Brandy
6 crêpes (see facing page)
½ cup brown sugar
1 pint vanilla ice cream or whipped cream

Combine 1 cup of sugar, coffee, dry spices, vanilla bean, and marmalade in a saucepan and simmer for 5 minutes over medium heat.

In a separate pan, sauté orange slices in 2 tablespoons of butter and remaining sugar for 2 minutes over medium-low heat.

Add brandy to the oranges and reduce by one-third.

Align crêpes on a plate and place warm orange slices evenly in the center of the crêpes and fold in half.

Melt the remaining butter and brown sugar in a large sauté pan. Add orange-stuffed crêpes and pour the coffee sauce over top; sauté for 1 minute over medium heat. Serve topped with ice cream or whipped cream.

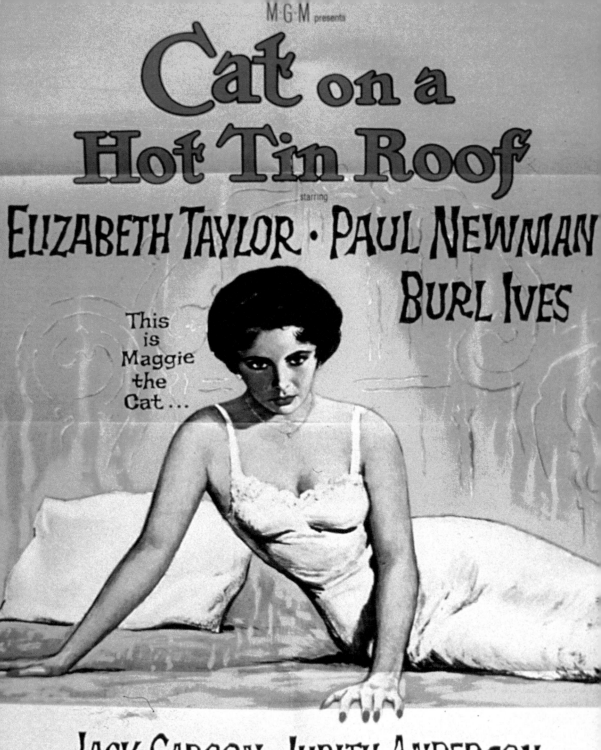

Left: *Cat on a Hot Tin Roof*
(1958)
Directed by Richard Brooks
Based on the play by
Tennessee Williams
Shown on the poster:
Elizabeth Taylor (as Margaret
'Maggie the Cat' Pollitt)

Right: Andy Warhol (left) and
Tennessee Williams (right)
talking on the S.S. France, 1967

RESTORATIVE AND MEDICINE

Frequently Williams uses the concept of liquor as medicinal in his plays. Most famously Brick in *Cat on a Hot Tin Roof* drinks Echo Springs bourbon to get the "click" that frees him from reality, or perhaps, as Big Daddy tells him, he does it "to kill your disgust with lying." Maggie recognizes the syndrome and says, "My daddy loved his liquor, he fell in love with his liquor the way you've fallin in love with Echo Springs." Even Big Daddy decides to have "a whiskey highball" in hopes of alleviating the terrible pain in his intestines. In *The Milk Train Doesn't Stop Here Anymore*, when the Witch of Capri arrives at the villa of her friend Flora Goforth, she is so shocked by the news that Christopher Flanders, known as the Angel of Death, is visiting there that she says, "I've got to have a wee spot of brandy on this!" Later, she tells Chris, "The shock I got last night when I—I had to drink myself blind!–when I saw her condition!" The landlady in *Vieux Carre*, after the trial in which she

has been convicted of disturbing the peace, offers the young writer a drink: "I only touch this bottle, which belonged to the late Mr. Wire, before he descended to hell between two crooked lawyers, I touch it only when forced to by such a shocking experience as I had tonight, the discovery that I was completely alone in the world, a solitary ole woman cared for by no one." In the same play, the artist named Nightingale keeps a bottle of white sherry in his room to ease him into sleep. In *Camino Real*, when Jacques Casanova goes into a rage after his long-overdue bill is presented, Gutman says, "Give him a thimble of brandy before he collapses. . . ." Jacques replies, "Here I sit, submitting to insults for a thimble of brandy. . . ." In the same play, Lord Byron discusses the decline of his poems as a result of the consumption of alcohol: "They seem to improve as the wine in the bottle—dwindles. *There is a passion for declivity in the world!*"

IN *A STREETCAR NAMED DESIRE,* BLANCHE ASKS

STELLA FOR A DRINK

"NO COKE, HONEY, NOT WITH MY NERVES TONIGHT! . . . JUST WATER, BABY TO CHASE IT! YOU DON'T GET WORRIED, YOUR SISTER HASN'T TURNED INTO

A DRUNKARD.

NIGHT OF
THE IGUANA

Grilled Ahi Tuna, Pineapple Relish, and Paneed Avocado

serves 6

RELISH
1 small pineapple
1/2 cup extra virgin olive oil, divided
Salt and pepper
1 small red onion, diced
2 ribs celery, diced
1 red bell pepper, diced
1 tablespoon minced tarragon
2 lemons, juiced

PANEED AVOCADO
2 ripe avocados, peeled, pitted, and quartered
Seasoned flour
Egg wash
Breadcrumbs
Peanut oil for frying

TUNA
6 (1- to 1½-inch-thick) center loin tuna steaks
Salt and pepper
1 pound spring mix greens
12 asparagus spears, steamed

Relish Peel, core, and slice pineapple. Season with a little extra virgin olive oil and salt and pepper; grill for 1 minute on each side. Let cool. Dice pineapple and place in a bowl with the vegetables and herbs. Add the citrus juice and remaining oil. Let mixture rest in a refrigerator for 1 hour prior to serving to allow flavors to meld.

Paneed Avocado Dust avocado in flour then dip in egg wash and then dredge in breadcrumbs. This procedure is best done in advance and refrigerated before deep frying. Deep fry avocado quarters in peanut oil at 350 degrees F until breading turns a golden brown.

Tuna Season tuna with salt and pepper and grill rare.

Assembly Using the juice from the relish, dress the greens and asparagus and place on the center of the plate. Place tuna on greens and top with relish. Arrange avocado on plate and serve.

Popcorn with Chili, Lime, Cebollitas, and Truffle Oil

serves 6

6 scallions
2 tablespoons extra virgin olive oil
Salt and pepper
1/2 lime, juiced
1 bag microwave popcorn
1 tablespoon dark chili powder
1 tablespoon white truffle oil

Toss the scallions in the oil and salt and pepper. Char on a grill, remove, and add the lime juice. Medium chop the scallions and set aside. Cook the popcorn according to package instructions. Toss the cooked popcorn with salt and pepper and the chili powder. Add the truffle oil and toss again. Add the scallions and serve as a great finger food.

Avocado, Grilled Calamari, and Garbanzo Bean Soup

serves 6

CALAMARI

12 large calamari with tentacles,
cleaned and grilled
Salt and pepper
1 tablespoon extra virgin olive oil

SOUP

2 large onions, medium chopped
1 large green bell pepper,
medium chopped
1 large red bell pepper,
medium chopped
1 medium jalapeño pepper,
finely diced
2 ribs celery, chopped
2 tablespoons extra virgin olive oil
2 cups white wine
1 tablespoon saffron threads
2 tablespoons minced garlic,
divided
3 roma tomatoes, chopped
2 quarts chicken stock
1 (8-ounce) can garbanzo beans
(or frozen if available)
1–2 medium ripe avocados,
peeled, pitted, and cubed

TOPPING

1½ cups sour cream
½ lime, juiced
1 teaspoon chopped parsley
1 teaspoon chopped cilantro
1 teaspoon Habanera Tabasco

Calamari Season the calamari with salt and pepper and toss in the olive oil. Grill each side for 1 minute or until nicely marked. Remove from the grill and slice into rounds. (Note: Squid will finish cooking perfectly in the hot broth, do not overcook on the grill.)

Soup Sauté the onions, bell peppers, and celery in the olive oil over low heat until lightly colored. Add white wine, saffron, 1 tablespoon garlic, and tomatoes and reduce for 2 minutes.

Add stock and beans; adjust seasoning with salt and pepper. Simmer for 10 minutes or until vegetables are tender. Add remaining garlic, grilled calamari, and avocado.

Topping In a separate bowl add the ingredients for topping together and whip. Spoon on top of hot soup in bowls. Serve with tortillas.

Lump Crabmeat, Grilled Pineapple, Poblano Pepper, and Grapefruit "Martini" with Smoked Garlic and Lime Vinaigrette

serves 6

VINAIGRETTE
10 cloves garlic, peeled
2 limes, juiced
2 tablespoons Dijon mustard
1/2 cup extra virgin olive oil
1 cup red wine vinegar
Salt and pepper

"MARTINI"
1 pound jumbo lump Louisiana Blue Crabmeat
4 leaves Romaine lettuce, chiffonade
6 slices pineapple
1 poblano pepper
2 ruby red grapefruit, peeled and segmented

Vinaigrette Cook whole cloves of garlic in a covered, salted water bath until tender. Drain and place garlic in a stovetop smoker or on an outside grill. Smoke until deep brown in color. Let cool, and then puree. Add lime juice and mustard. Slowly add olive oil and vinegar to the mixture to emulsify. Adjust seasoning with salt and pepper.

"Martini" Lightly dress the crabmeat and lettuce with the vinaigrette; keep separate. Flame the pineapple and poblano. Cut the pineapple into chunks and finely dice the poblano; mix together. Place on top of lettuce with the grapefruit and crabmeat and serve.

Pan-Seared Scallops with Roasted Corn, Cilantro, Tarragon, and Langoustine Cream

serves 6

2 ears corn in husks
3 cups heavy cream
1 teaspoon Habanera Tabasco
1 tablespoon Worcestershire sauce
1 teaspoon minced garlic
2 tablespoons chopped tarragon
1 tablespoon chopped cilantro
1 pound Louisiana crawfish or
Langoustine, cut in 1-inch pieces
Salt and pepper
18 jumbo scallops
Extra virgin olive oil
2 tablespoons unsalted butter
The Only Proper Mash Potatoes
with Truffle Oil (see facing page)

Roast the corn at 450 degrees F for 30 minutes with husks on. Remove, cool, and cut kernels from the cob. Combine corn, cream, Tabasco, Worcestershire, and garlic in a heavy saucepan. Cook for 4–5 minutes over medium-low heat. Add the tarragon and cilantro. Add the crawfish and adjust seasoning with salt and pepper to taste.

Heat a large flat-bottomed sauté pan to very hot. Season scallops with salt and pepper and a little bit of extra virgin olive oil. When pan is extremely hot, drop in the butter and quickly add the scallops. Let cook for 2 minutes on each side.

Place the scallops on a bed of the crawfish cream. Serve with the mashed potatoes.

The Only Proper Mash Potatoes with Truffle Oil

**"EVERYONE CAN DO MASH POTATOES,
BUT THERE IS ONLY ONE CORRECT WAY."**

serves 6

4 large potatoes, peeled
2 tablespoons kosher salt
1/2 teaspoon freshly ground pepper
8 tablespoons unsalted butter
1 tablespoon white truffle oil

Cut the potatoes into as symmetrical sizes or cubes as possible. Place in a large pot of very cold water with the salt. Water should be 4 times the amount of the potatoes. Bring to a boil and cook for 12–15 minutes, or until potatoes are tender. Pierce with a fork to check doneness; fork should go all the way to the center. Drain and place in a mixer with a whip attachment. Add the pepper and butter and whip, starting on low and moving to high, for 2–3 minutes. Drizzle the white truffle oil while whipping.

Grilled Swordfish with Black Beans, Chorizo, and Smoked-Gouda Rice Drizzled with a Tequila-Lime Beurre Blanc and Served with Cilantro, Mango, and Red Pepper Salad

serves 6

SWORDFISH

6 (4-ounce) swordfish portions
Salt and pepper
1 teaspoon minced garlic
2 tablespoons extra virgin olive oil
½ lemon, juiced

BLACK BEANS WITH CHORIZO AND
SMOKED-GOUDA RICE

6–8 ounces dry black beans
Water
1 pound chorizo sausage
1 quart chicken stock
2 ribs celery, chopped
1 large green bell pepper, chopped
1 tablespoon minced garlic
1 tablespoon dark chili powder
2 teaspoons cumin
2 cups uncooked jasmine rice
1½ cups cubed smoked Gouda
cheese
2 tablespoons chopped fresh
cilantro

Swordfish Season the swordfish with salt and pepper and marinate in the garlic and olive oil for 2–3 minutes. Grill on each side for 2 minutes, remove, and drizzle with lemon juice. Set aside.

Black Beans with Chorizo and Smoked-Gouda Rice Soak the black beans in water for 2 hours. Add all ingredients other than the rice, cheese, and cilantro and cook in a large pot until the beans are tender, about 2–4 hours over medium heat.

Cook rice according to the directions and when rice is tender remove to a sauté pan; add 2 cups of the bean and sausage mixture using a slotted spoon to let a lot of the liquid escape. Add the cubed cheese and toss together over low heat. Adjust seasoning with salt and pepper and add the cilantro.

2 cups white wine
2 tablespoons tequila
1 tablespoon heavy cream
1/2 lime, juiced
1/2 cup unsalted butter
Salt and pepper

SALAD
1 large red bell pepper
1 lemon, juiced
1 lime, juiced
1 tablespoon minced garlic
1 tablespoon chopped cilantro
Salt and pepper
1 mango, sliced
6 romaine leaves, torn into pieces

Tequila Beurre Blanc In a heavy-bottomed pan, place the wine and tequila over high heat and reduce au sec or by about two-thirds. Add the cream and lime juice. Melt butter and add to cream mixture to form the emulsion; whip the mixture vigorously while drizzling in the butter. Do this until the sauce is smooth and then immediately remove from heat.

Salad Grill the bell pepper and then deseed and slice. Whisk the juice of the lemon and lime with the garlic, cilantro, and salt and pepper. Toss with the bell pepper, mango slices, and lettuce.

Assembly Place the salad on a plate and the fish on top drizzled with the beurre blanc. Place the beans and rice on the side and serve.

Filet of Beef Tip Stroganoff with Carta Blanca Beer, Mushrooms, and Sour Cream

serves 6

3 pounds beef tenderloin tips
Salt and pepper
Flour, seasoned
$\frac{1}{2}$ cup oil
1 (12-ounce) bottle Carta Blanca beer
$\frac{1}{2}$ cup chopped onion
2 teaspoons minced garlic
1 pound domestic mushrooms, sliced
1 (8-ounce) can beef stock
$\frac{1}{2}$ cup veal demi-glace (optional)
1 cup sour cream
1 tablespoon chopped parsley
Cooked butter egg noodles, warm

Season tenderloin tips with salt and pepper and dust with seasoned flour. Sauté over high heat in the oil for 1 minute on both sides or until colored a light brown. Deglaze the beef with beer and remove with a slotted spoon, leaving the remaining juice in the pan. Add the onion, garlic, and mushrooms and sauté briefly before adding the beef stock and demi-glace, if using.

Simmer and reduce until the mushrooms and onions are tender. Return the meat back to the sauce and cook for 3 minutes or until medium-rare. Stir in sour cream and remove from heat. Serve over butter egg noodles and garnish with parsley.

CHEF to cook

Filet works best for this as it is faster to prepare and more tender.

"Rum Coco Tart" or Coconut in Shortbread Crust with Caramelized Bananas and Rum Caramel Sauce

serves 6

SHORTBREAD
1 cup flour
¼ teaspoon salt
¼ teaspoon cinnamon
1 tablespoon unsalted butter, cut into cubes
½ teaspoon vanilla

RUM COCO CREAM
2 cups coconut flakes
3 cups heavy cream
1 vanilla bean, split
1 cup sugar
4 egg yolks, beaten

CARAMEL
½ cup pineapple juice
1 cup sugar
2 cups heavy cream
2 tablespoons rum

BANANAS
2 bananas, sliced or diagonally sliced 1 inch thick
1 cup sugar in the raw

Shortbread Combine flour, salt, and cinnamon together in a food processor, pulse, and then add butter cubes and vanilla. Process ingredients together, pulsing until a semi-smooth dough forms. Do not overprocess. Remove and form into a ball. Refrigerate 1 hour or overnight. Slice dough into ⅛-inch slices, and form a crust into a pie dish. Bake at 350 degrees F for 5 minutes.

Rum Coco Cream Combine all the ingredients except the yolks and cook over medium heat for 12 minutes or until two-thirds thickened. Remove and scrape vanilla bean pod. Cool to room temperature. Fold in the yolks. Spread evenly over the prebaked shortbread. Bake at 400 degrees F for 10 minutes, remove, and let cool.

Caramel In a heavy, large, deep-sided saucepan over medium-high heat, reduce the pineapple juice to 1 or 2 tablespoons. Use a fork and combine the juice with the sugar and mix until it appears as wet sand. Cook again over medium-high heat. Do not stir, but lightly shake pan until mixture becomes an even caramel color, about 4–6 minutes. Be careful not to burn. Immediately add the cream. This will foam up, so be sure to use a large pot. Stir for 2–5 minutes, or until smooth and slightly thickened. Remove from heat and add the rum.

Bananas Place the bananas on a flameproof pan. Sprinkle generously with the sugar. Use a portable propane torch and "brûlé" the sugar until a golden caramel color.

Assembly Place a slice of coconut shortbread on a plate. Top with the bananas and drizzle the warm caramel sauce around the plate. Serve.

CAT ON A HOT
TIN ROOF

Pecan-Crusted Sweet Potato Pone with Gingered Peaches

serves 6 to 8

3 large sweet potatoes,
peeled and sliced
10 tablespoons unsalted butter,
divided
2 cups sugar, divided
2 teaspoons lemon juice
3 teaspoons vanilla extract
1 tablespoon cinnamon
¼ teaspoon nutmeg
2½ tablespoons cornstarch
⅓ cup milk
2 extra large eggs
1 large ripe peach, peeled, and
cut into ¼-inch cubes
1 teaspoon ginger
2 cups pecans, lightly crushed
½ cup confectioners' sugar

Boil the sweet potatoes until soft. Drain well and mash with 8 tablespoons butter, 1¼ cups sugar, lemon juice, vanilla extract, cinnamon, nutmeg, cornstarch, and milk; let cool. Slightly beat in the eggs and set mixture aside.

Sauté the peaches in a skillet with 1 tablespoon butter, ¼ cup sugar, and ginger until just tender and lightly browned. Fold into the sweet potato mixture.

Toss the pecans in remaining butter, melted, and remaining sugar. Spread the sweet potato mixture evenly into an 8 x 8-inch casserole dish and press a layer of the pecans on top. Bake at 350 degrees F for 1 hour. Begin checking periodically after 45 minutes with a toothpick. If the dish is firm and the toothpick comes out clean, then remove casserole from oven. Cool slightly and dust with the confectioners' sugar. This dish can be served warm from the oven or sliced into squares and served at room temperature or even cold.

Hoppin' John

serves 6

6 slices apple-smoked bacon
4 ounces smoked ham, cut into
1/2-inch cubes
2 tablespoons butter
2 ribs celery, chopped
1 medium onion, chopped
1 green bell pepper, chopped
3 tablespoons peanut oil
2 cups (16 ounces) cooked field
peas or black-eyed peas
3 teaspoons minced garlic
2 teaspoons fresh thyme
2 tablespoons chopped green
onions
1/2 cup chopped Italian flat-leaf
parsley
1 tablespoon Worcestershire sauce
1 cup veal demi-glace
3 cups cooked long-grain rice
Salt and pepper

Cook the bacon in an oven until crispy, remove to paper towels to drain, and reserve the bacon fat. Crumble bacon. Sauté the cubed ham in butter until light brown and set aside. Sauté the celery, onion, and bell pepper in the oil and bacon fat until tender.

Add the peas, garlic, thyme, green onions, parsley, Worcestershire, and demi-glace and cook for 3 minutes over medium heat. Add the cooked rice and warm through. Add ham and the crumbled crispy bacon and warm for 1–2 minutes more, until the ingredients resemble a jambalaya or rice pilaf. Season with salt and pepper to taste and serve.

Louisiana Frog Legs Grillade-Style with Bacon and Cheddar Grits and Poached Eggs

serves 4 to 6

FROG LEGS
2–4 legs per person, depending on size
Salt and pepper
All-purpose flour
3 tablespoons peanut oil
2 large onions, finely diced
2 ribs celery, finely diced
1 green bell pepper, finely diced
3 cups veal demi-glace (or 9 cups beef stock, reduced to 3 cups)
3 cloves minced garlic
3 tablespoons lite soy sauce
1 tablespoon tamarind paste
2 large ripe tomatoes, peeled, seeded, and finely chopped
2 teaspoons minced parsley

BACON AND CHEDDAR GRITS
4 cups freshly cooked grits
6–8 strips bacon, cooked until crispy
1 cup shredded cheddar cheese
2 poached eggs per person

Frog Legs Season frog legs with salt and pepper and then dust lightly with flour. Sauté legs briefly in hot peanut oil until lightly browned. Remove from pan, drain two-thirds of oil from pan, and then return pan to heat.

Add the onion, celery, and bell pepper; sauté over medium heat for 5–10 minutes. Add demi-glace, garlic, soy sauce, tamarind, tomatoes, and parsley; let simmer over medium-low heat for 15–20 minutes until vegetables are cooked. Season with salt and pepper to taste. Return legs to pan and cook 10 minutes more over low heat until medium-rare. Don't overcook the legs as they may become tough.

Bacon and Cheddar Grits Make 4 cups cooked grits according to package directions. While grits are very hot, add cooked bacon and cheese, then keep covered until ready to assemble dish.

Poach eggs, 2 per person, by cracking eggs in a simmering pot of 6 parts water to 1 part rice vinegar. Cook until whites are set and yolks are warm.

Assembly Place grits in center of plates, spoon frog legs and sauce onto grits, top with poached eggs, and serve.

Three Greens with Pickled Pork and Andouille Sausage

serves 6

1 pound Andouille sausage
1½ pounds pickled pork, cubed
3 tablespoons olive oil
1 large onion, chopped
1 large green bell pepper, chopped
2 ribs celery, chopped
1 bulb fennel, chopped
4–6 cups chicken stock
2 tablespoons Worcestershire sauce
1 tablespoon Creole mustard
1 large bunch mustard greens or kale
1 large bunch collard greens
2 tablespoons minced garlic
Salt and pepper
1 large bunch arugula

Roast the Andouille in an oven at 350 degrees F until cooked. Drain on paper towels and then slice into ½-inch cubes and set aside.

Sear the cubed pickled pork in oil until browned. Add the onion, bell pepper, celery, and fennel and stir constantly for 3 minutes. If the vegetables begin to stick to the bottom of the pan, add a little chicken stock. Cook until the vegetables are softened. Add remaining chicken stock, Worcestershire, and mustard and simmer for 40 minutes, until the pickled pork is very tender.

Add mustard and collard greens and let simmer, covered, for 15–30 minutes. When greens are tender but still bright, remove lid and cook uncovered with garlic, salt, and pepper to reduce the "pot liquor." Add cooked sausage and arugula and cook for 5 minutes more. Serve.

Poor as Job's Turkey

serves 6 to 8

1 turkey (10–12 pounds)
Salt and fresh ground pepper
½ cup peanut oil
2 carrots, peeled and chopped
4 ribs celery, chopped
2 large onions, chopped
1 head garlic, peeled and sliced
2 cups chicken stock
1 pound orzo pasta, dry

Cut turkey into 8 pieces, leaving bones in, and season with salt and pepper. Sauté in oil until golden on all sides. Remove the turkey and discard all excess oil, then add the chopped vegetables and garlic and sauté for 2–3 minutes. Add the stock and turkey back into the pan and cook, covered, over medium heat for 1 hour. Check periodically for doneness. If the liquid has become too reduced, add more stock or water.

When bird is tender, add orzo to pot and cook, covered, about 15 minutes or until pasta is cooked. Season with salt and pepper and serve.

CHEF to cook

This recipe came about as a result of Chef Greg being stranded at his home in Faubourg St. John in New Orleans after Hurricane Katrina. For the first few days, he used his frozen turkey as a giant ice cube, but it eventually defrosted. Forced to then cook it, he made do with what was on hand in his kitchen.

Big Daddy's Braised Double-Cut Pork Chops with Coca-Cola, Bourbon, Molasses, and Granny Smith Apples

serves 6

6 double-cut pork chops
Salt and pepper
2 cups flour, seasoned
½ cup olive oil
1 large onion, sliced
2 cups bourbon
4 cups Coca-Cola
2 cups apple juice
1 tablespoon minced garlic
3 tablespoons lite soy sauce
2 tablespoons Steen's Molasses
2 teaspoons Tabasco or Crystal Hot Sauce
2 cups demi-glace
2 tablespoons chopped fresh thyme
1 teaspoon chopped fresh rosemary
1 cup beef stock, if necessary
5 Granny Smith apples, cored and quartered

Season chops with salt and pepper and then dust in seasoned flour. Sear chops in hot oil in an ovenproof pan until they turn a light brown, about 2 minutes on each side, and remove to a plate. Carefully pour off excess oil from the pan and then add the onion and sauté for 2 minutes. Return the chops to pan and deglaze with the bourbon, allowing the pot liquor to reduce by two-thirds.

Add Coca-Cola, apple juice, garlic, soy sauce, molasses, Tabasco, demi-glace, thyme, rosemary, and salt and pepper. While cooking, take a brush and baste the chops every 5 minutes or so. Braise in an oven, uncovered, at 450 degrees F for 8 minutes. If needed, add stock or water if the "pot liquor" reduces too quickly. Reduce heat and cook at 350–400 degrees F for 20 minutes; turn the chops. Cook for an additional 20 minutes and then turn again. Add apples and cook an additional 20–40 minutes, until the meat is almost falling off the bone. Serve.

Candied Yam Bisque with Italian Sausage and Spiced Candied Pecans

serves 12

CANDIED YAM BISQUE WITH ITALIAN SAUSAGE

1–2 pounds Italian sausage
3 large onions, chopped
3 ribs celery, chopped
2 green medium bell peppers, chopped
2 carrots, peeled and chopped
3 tablespoons olive oil
¼ teaspoon garam marsala
2 teaspoons dark chili powder
¼ teaspoon cayenne pepper
1 tablespoon Chinese 5-spice powder
1 teaspoon dried lavender flowers
7 large yams, peeled and sliced
2 cups sherry
6 quarts chicken stock
2 tablespoons Worcestershire sauce
3 tablespoons soy sauce
2 cups freshly squeezed orange juice
2 tablespoons minced garlic
1 tablespoon tamarind paste*
2 cups heavy cream (optional)
Salt and pepper to taste
Spiced Candied Pecans (see next page)
4 scallions, sliced diagonally with white and green separated

This can be found at specialty markets.

Candied Yam Bisque with Italian Sausage Roast the sausage in the oven until cooked, remove, and drain well on paper towels; slice and set aside. Sauté the onions, celery, bell peppers, and carrots in oil until the onions turn translucent and there is a hint of brown coloring on all. Add the dry spices and sauté together until you can smell the spices rising from the pan. Add the yams and deglaze with the sherry. Sauté briefly before removing to a large pot.

In the stockpot add the stock, Worcestershire, soy sauce, orange juice, garlic, and tamarind paste. Simmer over medium-low heat for 1½ hours until the ingredients soften. Remove from heat and let cool slightly.

Remove several batches at a time and puree until smooth. Pass entire mixture through a fine strainer. Add the sausage to the pureed mixture and return to low heat in the pot. Let simmer for 5 minutes. Add the cream, if using, and salt and pepper to taste. Garnish with candied pecans and the green scallion tops and serve.

CHEF to cook

Butternut or acorn squash can be substituted for the yams.

SPICED CANDIED PECANS

1 egg white
2 dozen pecan halves
1½ teaspoons Tabasco or Crystal Hot Sauce
1 teaspoon Worcestershire sauce
1 cup sugar in the raw
1 teaspoon chili powder
1 teaspoon garlic powder
Salt and pepper

Spiced Candied Pecans Whip egg white until frothy (about 2 minutes by hand). Combine all the remaining ingredients in a separate bowl. Mix with egg white until the pecans are coated well. Let rest for 10 minutes.

Heat convection or regular oven to 400 degrees F. Stir mixture again, ensuring that nuts are well coated. Place pecans on a sheet pan that has been sprayed with nonstick spray and that is large enough to allow the nuts to be spread out. Bake for 3–7 minutes and then allow to cool before garnishing the bisque.

Lola's Cornbread

serves 8 to 10

1¼ cups all-purpose flour
1¼ cups self-rising cornmeal
1½ teaspoons baking powder
¼ cup sugar
1 teaspoon kosher salt
½ cup 2-percent milk
1½ cups half-and-half
2 eggs, beaten
¾ cup unsalted butter, melted
Butter for serving
Steen's Molasses for serving

Place a cast-iron skillet in a preheated 400-degree-F oven and let get very hot while making the batter.

Combine the dry ingredients in a bowl, then whisk in the milk, half-and-half, eggs, and butter. The mixture should resemble thick pancake batter or heavy cream. If too thick, thin by adding a little more milk.

Carefully pour batter into hot skillet and return to the oven to bake for 10–20 minutes. When bread is golden, check for doneness by inserting a toothpick in the center. If toothpick comes out clean, carefully remove the skillet and let rest for 2 minutes. Cut into squares and serve with butter and Steen's Molasses.

TENNESSEE WILLIAMS
A STREETCAR NAMED DESIRE

RECURRENT FOOD
AND DRINK

What food appears more often than any other in Tennessee's plays? Oddly enough, spaghetti, perhaps because, as several of his friends reported, it was one of the few things that he himself could and did cook. In a letter to his mother from the University of Iowa in 1938, he reported that he was sharing an apartment with another student and they were cooking for themselves: "we got six eggs for a dime and last night had a swell steak and spaghetti dinner for a total expenditure of forty cents." In one early play, *Not about Nightingales*, the fact that the prison keeps feeding their inmates spaghetti precipitates the hunger strike that leads to the final cataclysm; and in *A Streetcar Named Desire*, Eunice, the upstairs neighbor, is furious because she made "the spaghetti dish" for her husband but ate it all up when he was late.

**THE GLASS MENAGERIE OFFERS THIS ADVICE:
"EAT FOOD LEISURELY, SON, AND REALLY ENJOY IT.
A WELL COOKED MEAL HAS
LOTS OF DELICATE FLAVORS
THAT HAVE TO BE HELD IN THE MOUTH FOR APPRECIATION.
SO CHEW YOUR FOOD AND GIVE YOUR SALIVARY GLANDS
A CHANCE TO FUNCTION."**

TOWERS' CORK & WOOD PENHOLDER

Desserts recur in the plays, and, not surprisingly given the Southern settings of many of them, ice cream and variations thereof predominate. In *Summer and Smoke*, Mrs. Winemiller, who either is deranged or pretends to be, demands to know "Where is the ice cream man?" and when her daughter goes off to get some, she calls out, "Strawberry, Alma, chocolate, chocolate and strawberry mixed! Nor vanilla." Later, the Rev. Winemiller says of his wife, "She was on her worst behavior. Stopped in front of the White Star Pharmacy on Front Street and stood there like a mule; wouldn't budge till I bought her an ice cream cone." In *Eccentricities of a Nightingale*, Alma promises her mother four times that if she will go upstairs and remain there, she will bring her fruitcake. In *Spring Storm*, at an auction of desserts made by young ladies of Port Tyler, Arthur pays a surprising eighty dollars for Heavenly Critchfield's coconut cake.

Of the drinks he includes in his plays, and there are many, the one that recurs most often is the old Southern standby, Coca-Cola. In *Twenty-Seven Wagons Full of Cotton*, Flora has a headache and wants "a dope," as Coca-Colas were often called in those days, and in *Spring Storm*, the protagonist, Heavenly Critchfield, frequently drinks Cokes. Blanche mentions the drink several times in *A Streetcar Named Desire*, as when she asks Stella to "Run to the drug-store and get me a lemon-coke with plenty of chipped ice in it!" A few scenes later, when Stella brings her a drink, she inquires, "Is that coke for me? . . . Why you precious thing, you. It is just coke?" When Stella inquires, "You mean you want a shot in it?" Blanche replies, in one of her best one-liners, "Well, honey, a shot never does a coke any harm." Explaining to Big Daddy how much he has hated being a sportscaster rather than a football player in recent years, Brick describes himself as "Drinkin' a coke, half bourbon, so I can stand it?"

Julia Reed writes that "When Southerners are not cooking or eating, we're talking about food, arguing about it, going to get it, taking it somewhere, or inviting people over to have it." She reports a charming anecdote about William Faulkner and Katherine Anne Porter dining in a famous Paris restaurant, when Faulkner remarked, "Back home, the butter beans are in, the speckled ones" and Porter, starring into space, muttered "Blackberries." What, I wonder, might Tennessee Williams have added had he been a third member of the group?

THE ROSE
TATTOO

Pork Loin Franchese

serves 6

6 (4–6 ounce) center-cut boneless pork cutlets
Salt and pepper
2 teaspoons ground nutmeg
2 eggs, whipped
1–1½ cups grated Parmesan cheese
2 cups flour, seasoned
1 cup extra virgin olive oil
2 teaspoons chopped fresh parsley
1 lemon, cut into 6 slices

Using a flat meat tenderizer, place the cutlets between two sheets of plastic wrap and pound to ⅛ inch thickness. Season with salt, pepper, and nutmeg.

Mix the whipped eggs with the cheese in a bowl. Dredge the cutlets in the seasoned flour, shake off excess, and then dip in egg mixture. Sauté the cutlets in enough hot oil (350 degrees F) to almost cover them. Sauté each side for 2 minutes or until golden and pork is medium-rare. Serve topped with parsley and a lemon slice.

Pasta Fagolé with Italian Sausage, Penne, and Parmesan-Reggiano

serves 6 to 8

3 large onions, medium chopped
4 ribs celery, medium chopped
1 red bell pepper, chopped
4 carrots, peeled and medium diced
1/2 cup extra virgin olive oil
6 quarts chicken stock
4 tablespoons minced garlic
3 tablespoons chopped parsley
1 pound cannellini beans, soaked overnight and drained (or canned)
Salt and pepper
2 pounds Italian sausage
2 tablespoons chopped rosemary
1/2 pound penne pasta, cooked al dente
5 ounces shaved Parmesan

Sauté the onions, celery, bell pepper, and carrots in oil for 3–4 minutes over low heat until the onions turn slightly translucent. Add stock, garlic, parsley, and beans and season with salt and pepper to taste. Let cook for 1–1½ hours or until beans are tender.

While the beans are cooking, place the sausage onto a sheet pan and roast until cooked. Remove and cool, then slice into circles and drain on paper towels to remove excess fat. Add the sausage to beans with the rosemary and cooked pasta. Place in a bowl, sprinkle with the Parmesan, and serve.

Spaghetti with Meatballs in Fennel and Sambuca Cream with Grape Tomatoes and Grapes

serves 6

MEATBALLS IN FENNEL AND SAMBUCA CREAM

2 tablespoons minced fennel bulb
3 tablespoons butter
2 teaspoons Sambuca
2 quarts chicken stock, divided
1 medium onion, minced
1 rib celery, minced
1 small green bell pepper, minced
2 tablespoons oil
1 pound lean ground beef
1/2 pound ground pork
1/2 pound ground veal
1 tablespoon Worcestershire sauce
1 tablespoon minced garlic, divided
1 tablespoon chopped parsley
1 teaspoon chopped fresh oregano
Salt and pepper
2 eggs, beaten
2 cups breadcrumbs
3 cups heavy cream

Meatballs in Fennel and Sambuca Cream Sauté fennel in butter for 3 minutes and then deglaze with the Sambuca. Add 1/2 cup chicken stock and cook over medium heat for 4 minutes, or until the fennel is tender. Remove fennel from the liquid and set aside. Reduce the sauce by half or until lightly thickened.

Sauté the onion, celery, and bell pepper in the oil for 6 minutes or until tender. Cool slightly, then add the beef, pork, veal, Worcestershire sauce, one-third of the garlic, herbs, and one-third of the cooked fennel.

Remove everything from the oil and place into a large bowl. In another bowl, mix the salt and pepper with the eggs; add the cheese and breadcrumbs, mixing well. Combine the breadcrumb mixture with the meat mixture, distributing ingredients evenly. Allow to cool more, then use either your hands or an ice cream scoop to form mixture into 30 small meatballs. Gently place the meatballs on a sheet pan that has been sprayed with nonstick spray and bake at 450 degrees F for 7–9 minutes, until brown and firm. Do not overbake. Once meatballs are cool, carefully remove excess fat and remove meatballs to paper towels to drain.

2 tablespoons chopped red onion
1 tablespoon extra virgin olive oil
4 roma tomatoes, chopped
1 tablespoon minced garlic
2 tablespoons chopped fresh parsley
Cooked pasta for serving
$1/2$ cup grated Parmesan cheese
4 medium roma tomatoes, diced
$1/2$ pound grapes, halved

Combine the remaining chicken stock, fennel stock, two-thirds cooked fennel, and cream in a sauté pot. Add the prebaked meatballs and finish cooking at a low simmer for 15–20 minutes, reducing the liquid by about half.

Pasta and Set-Up Sauté the onion in oil until lightly brown. Add the chopped tomatoes, garlic, parsley, and the reduced fennel cream from meatballs. Cook for 3 minutes over medium-low heat until the vegetables are tender. Cook pasta of your choice, preferably linguine, to al dente. Drain the pasta and add to the sauce. Toss in cheese, diced tomatoes, and grape halves. Add the meatballs and serve.

Fontina and Banana Arancini

serves 6

3 tablespoons butter
1 cup uncooked Arborio rice
1 cup white wine
6 cups water
1 large pinch salt
2 tablespoons brown sugar
1/2 cup sugar
2 teaspoons ground cinnamon
1/2 teaspoon ground cloves
1 teaspoon ground nutmeg
1 banana, mashed
1 cup cream
1 teaspoon vanilla extract
1 banana, cubed
4 ounces fontina goat cheese, cut
into 6 cubes

BREADING AND SET-UP
3 cups all-purpose flour
Egg wash
3 cups unseasoned breadcrumbs
6 cups peanut oil for frying
Confectioners' sugar for dusting

Melt the butter in a heavy-bottomed skillet and sauté the dry rice; deglaze with the wine. Add the water 1 cup at a time and cook, allowing water to reduce before adding more water. Add the salt. Stir constantly over high heat until the rice is tender.

Add the sugars, spices, mashed banana, and cream. Cook together for 2–3 minutes; add the vanilla and remove from heat. Let cool completely and then refrigerate for 1 hour.

Fold the cubed banana into the risotto. Roll spoonfuls of the risotto into 3-inch balls and poke 1 piece of cheese into each ball with your finger. Roll ball smooth. Cover balls lightly with plastic wrap and refrigerate for 6 hours, until very cold and set.

Breading and Set-Up Handling the risotto balls very gently (as they may break), dredge the balls in flour, then dip into the egg wash, and then dredge in the breadcrumbs. Refrigerate for 1 hour.

Heat peanut oil to 375 degrees F. Carefully fry until the balls become golden brown. Remove and drain excess oil from the balls on paper towels. Dust with confectioners' sugar and serve with a dark beer as a dessert.

Rose-Scented Spumante Ice Cream Soda with Grappa Flambé Grapes

serves 6

1 pound green seedless grapes, halved
2 teaspoons sugar
2 cups Grappa
1 pint lemon gelato
6 tablespoons rose water or rose nectar
1 bottle Spumante, chilled
6 sprigs fresh mint

Place grape halves with sugar and Grappa in a sauté pan. Place over high heat, being careful as this will flame up. Tip edge very carefully to flame to catch the Grappa on fire. Flame grapes and then remove from heat and set aside to ensure that Grappa has completely burned out.

Place 2 scoops of the gelato into each of six large soda glasses, and divide and add the rose water evenly between the glasses. Divide the chilled Spumante into the soda glasses and top with the flamed grapes and sprigs of mint.

Bag of Chocolate Truffles with Marsala Raisins

makes 24

1 pound Belgium bittersweet
chocolate
1¾ cups heavy cream
2 tablespoons unsalted butter
⅛ cup sugar
1 cup water
1 cup Marsala wine
24 golden raisins
1–1½ cups Hershey's
unsweetened cocoa

Chop the chocolate as evenly as possible and then place into a stainless steel bowl. In a sauté pot, heat the cream, butter, and sugar to a boil and then carefully pour over the chopped chocolate. Cover with plastic wrap and let stand for 7 minutes.

Remove plastic wrap and whip the ingredients until thoroughly mixed and smooth. Divide the mixture into thirds; set aside one-third and refrigerate two-thirds of the mixture for 24 hours.

Heat the water with the Marsala wine and then pour over the golden raisins in a bowl. Allow to rehydrate for 10 minutes and then drain and let air-dry.

Reheat the reserved one-third chocolate mixture for dipping for 30 seconds in the microwave. Out of the refrigerated chocolate, roll little 1½-inch diameter balls and place a single raisin in the center of each ball. Smooth chocolate around raisin in ball and set out on parchment paper. Continue this until all of the refrigerated chocolate is used up; you should have about 2 dozen balls.

Dip each ball into the warm chocolate sauce and roll in cocoa powder. Place on parchment paper until serving.

THE TENNESSEE WILLIAMS DINNER

Waldorf Salad with Golden Raisins, Pistachio Nuts, Celery, Caramelized Yams, and Goat Cheese Vinaigrette

serves 6

NUTS AND YAMS
4 tablespoons pistachio nuts, shelled
3 tablespoons extra virgin olive oil, divided
Salt and pepper
1–1½ pounds yams

GOAT CHEESE VINAIGRETTE
½ cup rice vinegar
½ cup extra virgin olive oil
1 teaspoon finely minced garlic
1 tablespoon finely minced parsley
1 teaspoon Worcestershire sauce
⅓ pound goat cheese
1 cup mayonnaise

SALAD
3 heads Belgian endive
2 ribs celery, diced
4 tablespoons golden raisins

Nuts and Yams Toast nuts in 1 tablespoon oil and season with salt and pepper; cook for 1 minute, being careful not to burn. Set aside and allow to cool.

Dice yams into 1-inch squares and blanche in boiling salted water until nearly tender; remove and drain. Toss the yams in remaining oil and season with salt and pepper. Place on a sheet pan in an oven preheated to 400 degrees F and roast until tender and golden brown. Remove and set aside to cool.

Goat Cheese Vinaigrette Combine and mix first 5 ingredients until emulsified. Incorporate the goat cheese and then add the mayonnaise and combine until smooth.

Assembly Remove the large outside leaves from the endive and reserve them for plating. Chiffonade the remaining endive. Toss the chiffonade endive, pistachio nuts, celery, yams, and raisins in the vinaigrette and place onto the reserved endive leaves; serve.

CHEF to cook

It was reported that a Waldorf Salad was a favorite of Tennessee Williams, but his doctor forbade him to eat it, especially the nuts.

Crawfish Callas with Horseradish Sabayon

CALLAS IS AN OLD CREOLE BREAKFAST ITEM; THIS IS A SAVORY VERSION.

makes 24 to 30

CALLAS AND FILLING
1 pound Louisiana crawfish tails, drained
Peanut oil for frying
1/2 teaspoon dried red pepper flakes
1 large onion, finely chopped
1 large green bell pepper, finely chopped
3 cloves garlic, minced
1 tablespoon dark chili powder
1 teaspoon cayenne pepper
Kosher salt and pepper
2 1/2 cups all-purpose flour
Pinch salt
1 tablespoon baking powder
3 eggs, beaten
1 1/2 cups cooked long-grain rice

SABAYON
7 egg yolks
1 cup Marsala wine
1 cup sugar
1 teaspoon Tabasco or Crystal Hot Sauce
1/2 cup prepared horseradish
1/2 lemon, juiced
2 cups heavy cream

Callas and Filling Sauté the crawfish in a sauté pot with a small amount of peanut oil and the dried pepper flakes for 1 minute; then let cool. Remove the crawfish with a slotted spoon and set aside. Add the vegetables and spices to the pot and sauté until tender. Return crawfish to the pot and toss and mix together thoroughly with vegetables; remove from heat and let cool.

In a separate bowl, combine the flour, a pinch of salt, baking powder, eggs, cooked rice, and vegetable-crawfish mixture. Mix thoroughly. Refrigerate for 1 hour. If using later, freeze the Callas now, before frying.

Roll the mixture into 2-inch balls and dry fry in peanut oil until golden brown. Set aside on paper towels.

Sabayon Make the Sabayon by whipping until smooth the egg yolks, Marsala, sugar, Tabasco, horseradish, and lemon juice in a clean bowl. Place in a double boiler and, using a heatproof spatula, stir mixture constantly being sure to scrape the sides, for 15 minutes, or until the mixture has thickened and is a bright yellow color.

Place mixture in a clean mixing bowl and whip on medium-high for 3 minutes. Add the cream in a slow and steady stream for another 1–2 minutes to emulsify. Do not overmix as the sauce may break apart. Serve warm over the callas.

Sautéed Veal Sweetbreads with Mushrooms, Caramelized Red Onions, and Blueberry Compote with Roasted Corn and Edamame "Succotash"

serves 6

SWEETBREADS
1 pound veal sweetbreads, sinew cleaned
1 quart beef stock

CARAMELIZED RED ONIONS
1 large red onion, sliced thinly
1 tablespoon extra virgin olive oil
1 cup balsamic vinegar
1/4–1/2 cup honey

SUCCOTASH
2 ears corn, in husks
1/2 cup chopped yellow onion
4 tablespoons butter
2 cups shelled edamame
1 tablespoon chopped fresh thyme
2 tablespoons minced garlic
Salt and pepper

ASSEMBLY
1 cup all-purpose flour
1 tablespoon extra virgin olive oil
2 tablespoons Madeira
3 tablespoons veal demi-glace
1 teaspoon minced garlic
1/2 pint blueberries
1/4 pound button mushrooms, diced
1 tablespoon unsalted butter
Salt and pepper

Sweetbreads Poach the sweetbreads in the beef stock at a medium simmer for 5–7 minutes until springy to the touch. Remove and place between two plates; weight top plate to compress the sweetbreads and let cool.

Caramelized Red Onions Sauté the onions in oil for 2 minutes, add the balsamic and honey, and reduce heat to low. Cook for 10–12 minutes, until the onions are cooked and the balsamic is reduced. Cool.

Succotash Roast the corn with husks on at 475 degrees F for 10 minutes. Let cool and then cut the corn from the cobs. Sauté the roasted corn with the onion for 2–3 minutes in the butter and then add the edamame, thyme, garlic, and salt and pepper. Cook for 1 minute.

Assembly Slice the sweetbreads into 1/2-inch slices, season with salt and pepper, and dust in flour. Heat sauté pan and add the olive oil; sauté sweetbreads for 30 seconds on each side. Deglaze with Madeira and then add the Caramelized Red Onions. Add the demi-glace and garlic. Remove from heat and add the blueberries. Cook mushrooms with butter and salt and pepper to taste over medium heat for 3–4 minutes. Add to sweetbreads. Arrange the succotash on a plate and top with the sweetbreads and sauce.

Pecan-Crusted Black Drum with Spinach Risotto and Creole Hollandaise

A DIFFERENT LOOK AT THE OLD NEW ORLEANS TROUT ALMONDINE.

serves 6

PECAN-CRUSTED BLACK DRUM
6 (5- to 6-ounce) filets black drum
Salt and pepper
2 eggs
2 cups half-and-half
1 cup all-purpose flour, seasoned
3 pounds pecans, processed into coarse flour
4 cups peanut oil

RISOTTO
1 large onion, chopped medium fine
2 teaspoons minced garlic
1 cup extra virgin olive oil, divided
1 pound uncooked Arborio rice
2 cups white wine
2–5 cups chicken stock
3 pounds spinach, cleaned

CREOLE HOLLANDAISE
4 tablespoons water
1 lemon, juiced
2 tablespoons white wine vinegar
2 tablespoons Creole mustard
6 large egg yolks
1 cup butter, cut into cubes
1/4 tablespoon cayenne pepper

Pecan-Crusted Black Drum Season the fish with salt and pepper. Make an egg wash by beating together the eggs, half-and-half, and salt and pepper. Dust fish in flour and then dredge in egg wash. Coat in the pecan flour and refrigerate until ready to fry.

Risotto Sauté the onion and garlic in 1 tablespoon olive oil for 2–3 minutes, until lightly colored. Add rice and toss in the oil with the onions. Deglaze with white wine. Cook over high heat, stirring in 1 cup of stock at a time, until the liquid is absorbed and the rice is tender. Add spinach.

Creole Hollandaise Combine the water, lemon juice, vinegar, and mustard in a large stainless steel bowl. Heat over a double boiler. Add the egg yolks and whisk until yolks turn a light lemon color. Add butter in four batches and whip sauce until triple in volume.

Assembly Heat the peanut oil to 375 degrees F and fry the fish for 3 minutes per side or until golden brown. Serve the fish over the risotto with a generous drizzle of the hollandaise sauce on top.

RECIPE INDEX

Metric Conversion Chart

Volume Measurements		Weight Measurements		Temperature Conversion	
U.S.	Metric	U.S.	Metric	Fahrenheit	Celsius
1 teaspoon	5 ml	½ ounce	15 g	250	120
1 tablespoon	15 ml	1 ounce	30 g	300	150
¼ cup	60 ml	3 ounces	90 g	325	160
⅓ cup	75 ml	4 ounces	115 g	350	180
½ cup	125 ml	8 ounces	225 g	375	190
⅔ cup	150 ml	12 ounces	350 g	400	200
¾ cup	175 ml	1 pound	450 g	425	220
1 cup	250 ml	2¼ pounds	1 kg	450	230

RESOURCES

Products for use in the recipes and special thanks:

THE BISTRO AT THE
MAISON DEVILLE

THE NEW ORLEANS TENNESSEE
WILLIAMS LITERARY FESTIVAL
938 Lafayette Street #514
New Orleans, LA 70113
504.581.1144
Tennesseewilliams.net

COLLECTION OF TENNESSEE
WILLIAMS

TABLEWARE, SILVER & LINENS

THE ESTATE OF VERNA MEYERS

CATHEAD VODKA
PO BOX 4917
Jackson, MS 39296
catheadvodka.com

NOLA BROWN ALE
New Orleans Lager and Ale
Brewing Company
3001 Tchoupitoulas Street
New Orleans, LA 70115
nolabrewing.com

STEEN'S MOLASSES
C. S. Steen's Syrup Mill, Inc.
P.O. Box 339
119 N. Main Street
Abbeville, LA 70510
steenssyrup.com

SOUTHERN PECAN NUT
BROWN ALE
Lazy Magnolia Brewery
P.O. Box 1476
Kiln, MS 39556
lazymagnolia.com

COMMUNITY COFFEE
Community Coffee Company
P.O. Box 2311
Baton Rouge, LA 70821
communitycoffee.com

GLASSWARE
Mignon Faget, Ltd.
3801 Magazine Street
New Orleans, LA 70115
mignonfaget.com

NOUVELLE-ORLÉANS
ABSINTHE SUPÉRIEURE
Jade Liqueurs
bestabsinthe.com

PEYCHOUD BITTERS
Sazerac, Co.
803 Jefferson Highway
New Orleans, LA 70121-2584
sazerac.com

HERBSAINT
Sazerac, Co.
803 Jefferson Highway
New Orleans, LA 70121-2584
sazerac.com

ANDOUILLE
Chef Paul Prudhomme
PO Box 23342
New Orleans, LA 70183-0342
chefpaul.com

COMEAUX'S CAJUN GROCER
709 Park Way Drive
Breaux Bridge, La 70517
cajungrocer.com

THE HISTORIC NEW ORLEANS
COLLECTION
533 Royal Street
New Orleans, LA 70130
504.523.4662
Hnoc.org

IRISH CHANNEL STOUT
New Orleans Lager and Ale
Brewing Company
3001 Tchoupitoulas Street
New Orleans, LA 70115
nolabrewing.com

BLUE BAYOU MUSCADINE WINE
Old South Winery
65 South Concord Avenue
Natchez, MS 39120
601.445.9924
Oldsouthwinery.com

About the Authors

Chef Greg Picolo operates a small upscale bistro located across a hidden French Quarter courtyard from where Tennessee Williams resided for years. The Bistro and Chef Greg have received numerous awards, appeared on the Food Network, and been featured in local and national periodicals and newspapers such as *Bon Appetite, Gourmet, Sante,* and *The New York Times.* The Bistro has been rated as one of "America's Top Restaurants" by Zagat. Chef Greg annually puts on Tennessee Williams themed menus during the Williams Literary Festival.

Dr. Kenneth Holditch, renowned Tennessee Williams scholar and research professor at the University of New Orleans, brings with him a remarkable wealth of new and existing essays related to food throughout Williams's work and life. Aside from his extensive academic credentials and numerous published works regarding Williams, Dr. Holditch knew Williams personally and through this holds a true understanding and link to the man.

A native of New Orleans, **Troy Gilbert** is a freelance journalist and author. His work for many national and regional publications covers investigative journalism, competitive sailing, and travel. *Dinner with Tennessee Williams* is his third book.